Have Yourself a

MINIMALIST

CHRISTMAS

Slow Down, Save Money &
Enjoy a More Intentional Holiday

meg nordmann

Ordering Information: Quantity sales. Special discounts are available on quantity purchases by corporations, associations, and others. For details, contact the publisher via the website address below.

www.MegNordmann.com

Printed in the United States of America

First Printing, 2020

(Hardcover)
ISBN 13: 978-1-7349121-2-8

(Paperback)
ISBN 13: 978-1-7349121-1-1

(Ebook)
ISBN 13: 978-1-7349121-0-4

(Audiobook)
ISBN 13: 978-1-7349121-3-5

Library of Congress Control Number:
2020913728

Contributors:

Cover & Interior Book Design by: Amy Evans-Vega

Editor: Amber Hatch

Foreword: Denaye Barahona, Ph.D.

Cover Illustration: Meg Nordmann

To my children,
who not only were the catalyst for me
seeking peace in minimalism, but also the
reason for pursuing my creative passions.
May this book one day inspire you to
chase all of your biggest dreams.

Table of Contents

foreword

When I was growing up in rural Ohio, Christmas was special. We were a working-class family and my parents worked hard all year to save money to buy as many gifts as they could afford. I remember the sleepless Christmas Eves waiting in anticipation of a morning spent tearing through packages. I have fun memories of those glorious mornings.

But as a result, my childhood goal during the holiday season was linear in focus—accumulate as many tangible gifts as possible and relish in the day of receiving. But that's really all I remember. I don't really remember the time I spent with my family. I don't really remember the religious celebration and sentiments. I don't remember *giving*.

I don't remember capturing the real reason for the season.

When the day after Christmas came, the buzz had worn off. I took my pile of new stuff to my messy bedroom where I added it onto the other piles of stuff that had come in years before it. And in all the years that were to come ahead, those piles only grew.

As the piles of stuff grew, so did my seeking of "the stuff." That became the goal of growing up: Study hard, get good grades, go to college, make a lot of money, buy as much stuff

1

as you can afford. Isn't that what success looks like? Because that's what society tells us.

It would be decades later when I finally realized the weight of all the stuff—the physical clutter would continue to accumulate and contribute to the mental clutter swirling around in my brain. As I became a mother myself, I cherished my childhood holiday memories, but I also knew that I wanted to shift the focus with my own family.

But learning new habits and making change doesn't come easily. It took me years of trial and error to figure out what minimalism meant for my family. That's why I'm thrilled that Meg has written this book to guide and partner with families to make the holiday season more meaningful.

In this book you'll find a blueprint for approaching the season with intention—it's something I wish I had for my family years ago.

This year, I'm wishing you a simpler and more intentional holiday season. With all the joy and less of the stuff.

Denaye Barahona, Ph.D.
Founder of the *Simple Families* brand and top-rated podcast
www.simplefamilies.com

Introduction

Does the thought of Christmas coming around the corner make you wince inside?

Are you imagining your bank account decreasing at a rapid rate? The stress of a tight month? The stress of not having enough money to get the things you want to purchase? The thought of budgeting necessities like groceries after making a huge Amazon purchase? Do you swallow a sickening gulp as you hear the total at the Target checkout? *How did that Dollar Section suddenly stack up to $100?*

Or is it the impending mess that fills you with dread? The thought of all that new stuff marching into your home? Where will you put it all? Who's going to clean it all up? And then clean it up again...constantly, perpetually?

You know who.

Or is it a lack of time that stresses you out? Do you worry about how you'll manage to squeeze in a visit to Santa? Or find time to bake cookies with your children? And decorate the house? And the tree? And do everything expected in just a matter of a few weekends? Does it feel like pure chaos? Is it all overwhelming?

Or is it the decorating that makes you groan? Do you dread hauling the heavy red and green boxes down from the attic?

Do the decorations, crammed onto already cluttered surfaces, make you feel claustrophobic after a week? Do you wait until Valentine's Day to finish packing it all up because it's just *too much* work to take down?

You are not alone.

I know these feelings well—because I've been there.

You shouldn't have to dread the "most magical time of the year."

It *can* be magical. You *can* achieve that.

The secret to finding that magic is in *doing and buying less.*

Less is more.

I'll guide you through cutting out the excess and getting back to the basics that really make for an enjoyable, intentional, simple, and stress-free holiday season with your family. Here are my practical steps for celebrating Christmas like a minimalist.

I recommend reading this book in the fall months leading up to December. If you can prepare your mindset, budget, calendar and your home in the months of September, October and November, then you will be well-prepared for a less expensive, more intentional and joyful holiday.

However, if you receive this book as a Christmas gift, I believe that many of these tips can still be useful and applicable for any time of the year. You may view holiday-specific action items and examples in a more general way to help simplify your life at any time of the year.

About the structure of this book:

Chapter 1 takes a look at the definition of a minimalist and some of the reasons we are naturally inclined to accumulate objects in an effort to fit into society—often to a level that has left us experiencing anxiety and overwhelm. I recount my own minimalist journey and how this applies specifically to the holiday season.

Chapter 2 explores the history of Christmas—in particular, the story around Santa Claus in the United States—to reveal just how young this consumerist tradition actually is. We also take a look at the Big Business behind Christmas in an effort to peel away the manipulative marketing and create a healthier mindset shift.

Chapter 3 dives into the practical steps for decluttering four specific areas of your home before the holidays arrive. This will help you make space for the inevitable influx of new items and create a calmer environment for holiday memories to be made.

Chapter 4 focuses on intentionality in two areas: simplifying your decorations and planning out your time for events and traditions. This chapter guides you in how to both budget and plan the pacing of these activities so that you and your family do not feel overwhelmed.

Chapter 5 discusses holiday traditions. In this chapter I give a list of simple traditions that encourage little to no spending with a focus on memory-making. It also gives you the permission you may need to start editing out existing traditions that may not be a good fit for your family. This will relieve the pressure of expectations and give your family a slower pace to enjoy what matters most.

Chapter 6 guides you through three strategies you can take to drastically cut the amount of gifts you purchase for Christmas, and why this matters. It answers several questions about how to achieve fewer gifts—particularly addressing your children's expectations.

Chapter 7 explores three ways to focus on becoming more in tune with the present moment, so you don't miss precious time with your family being distracted by constant competition for your attention.

Chapter 8 navigates three strategies for getting your extended family and close friends on board with your minimalist goals. It also sets realistic expectations for the well-meaning gift-givers who may not understand your new goals for having and doing "less."

Chapter 9 guides you through yet another decluttering round as you find space for new items and settle into your new normal—a peaceful home—after the holidays have ended.

Throughout this book I refer to Christmas and the holiday season interchangeably to remain inclusive of all traditions that occur in the months of December and January. At Christmas, Christians celebrate the birth of Jesus. The festival has also become a major *cultural* tradition, celebrated by believers and non-believers alike. The commercialization of Christmas has overwhelmed the season and its traditional spirit of goodwill and togetherness. This book is written for those readers who want to reduce that excess and reclaim a simpler, more special experience, whether that includes a spiritual element or not.

If you start from the beginning of this book you will get an understanding of minimalism and the mindset shifts needed—towards your items, your time, and the consumerist origins of this holiday—before diving into the more practical steps like decluttering and implementing guidelines around gifts. But it's also okay to read the chapters in whatever order would make the most sense for your needs.

1

WHAT IS MINIMALISM? HOW DOES IT APPLY TO CHRISTMAS?

Minimalism is a lifestyle that embraces less and focuses on keeping only the necessary so that you can achieve a more peaceful and joyful existence. Decluttering is the act of paring down your belongings (tangible or intangible) to the essentials that you use, need and love. This is something that you can work towards on your own, or as a family unit. You shouldn't expect to do this all at once: a lot of the work is internal and it takes time to shift your mindset.

Our genetics have hardwired us to become proud collectors of material things, and thousands of years of programming are embedded in us to seek approval from society. As far back as our caveman days, we worked to be accepted into the safety of the "tribe" to keep from being left outside of the cave, susceptible to life-threatening predators and inclement weather. We still seek that approval. Furthermore, our brains get a chemical cocktail boost of dopamine when we obtain a new item, and like a drug, we seek more and more of that feel-good chemical to feel happy or satisfied.

We are emotional beings, and shedding sentimental items can be incredibly difficult. Our consumerist society, fueled by brilliant marketing, has convinced us that we need more stuff, new stuff, better stuff, bigger stuff, and to accumulate it at any cost—even deep debt with high interest. Sunk-cost-bias holds us back from purging unnecessary items because we just can't face the painful fact that we wasted all of that money. We often attach an inflated value to items, ignoring that the *true* value (what someone else would pay for it) is substantially less than our perceived value, if nothing at all. Yet we continue to hold onto the idea that our items are still worth something, even long after they have stopped giving us any benefit. We're all guilty of some form of hoarding. We can't seem to help ourselves from collecting. And the next thing we know, we find ourselves overwhelmed by the sheer amount of items in our space and the task of storing, managing, moving and cleaning these items.

This overwhelm turns into anxiety and the constant stream of cortisol (stress hormone) being released into our body is the root of most health problems. We work more in order to pay for our stuff's debt or storage space. Because we are working so hard to pay for our stuff, and then working so hard to clean and manage all of our stuff, we are unable to find as much time as we would like to spend with our family or on the passion projects that matter the most to us. It's so easy to get stuck in this loop, and quite frankly, all of this stuff is *stealing* from us. It's stealing our health, our money, our time, and our joy.

And this theft is particularly rampant around the holidays, as so much of this season centers around giving and receiving more stuff, as well as *doing* more stuff.

Christmas can be a time of great joy with its beautifully decorated sights, incredible smells, cheerful salutations and carols. The crispness in the air and the fresh fallen snow probably triggers happy childhood memories. But it's so easy for it to get away from us. The busyness and the consumerism overshadows the season's magic and we can easily get swept up in the good deals. We might feel the urge to go shopping for "the next best thing" and get "the perfect gift" for everyone we know. We might feel compelled to decorate a "Pinterest Perfect," "Instagram-Worthy" home, subconsciously competing with or emulating online influencers and glossy magazines. We can cram too much into our schedules and end up with stressed and uncooperative families. That initial joy gets zapped by trying to do All The Things and getting All The Stuff.

Of course, the irony is that this is the complete opposite of what we all intended the holidays to be about. Regardless of religions or philosophies, we all know that the meaning behind Christmas is about togetherness. It's about acts of kindness and good cheer. It's about joy and peace. We can achieve that by slowing down and simplifying.

My hope is that after reading this book you find the will-power, mindset shift and tactical advice to help you and your family do exactly that.

MY MINIMALIST JOURNEY

Before going any further, let me introduce myself and give a quick history of my own journey to minimalism. Ten years ago, I lived in a large 1,600-square foot home filled with heavy antiques and abstract paintings. I was not a fan of the chaotic art, but my spouse had inherited the collection from his mother. The furniture was dark and the space felt both busy and cavelike. I felt uncomfortable in my own home. I had two entire closets devoted to my clothes alone, and shoe racks lined an entire wall of the guest bedroom. I considered myself a "collector" of shoes. A week did not go by where I wasn't cramming more new clothes onto hangers in one of the closets. In fact, my in-laws even gifted me more hangers for Christmas one year.

I felt like I "deserved" something nice after a hard week's work, so to have something to show for it, I bought another trinket for my house or closet. But the happiness I received from obtaining the new item would quickly fade and it would be shoved to the side for next week's hard-earned prize. I allowed myself to think I was so important that I couldn't possibly be seen wearing the same thing twice. My publishing job kept me at society and arts events nearly every evening, so I felt pressure to constantly "wow" everyone with the newest, most fashionable clothes. Since each event was captured on social media, I would wait an entire year before wearing an outfit a second time. I said "yes" to every single event invitation extended to me. Every evening was an opportunity, and I valued networking and my place in society. Some nights I would attend three different events, often with a "costume change" between each one. I became known as a "yes girl" and my abilities to network for others and provide interesting coverage in the local newspapers and magazines made my email inbox and social media accounts very popular. I often felt overwhelmed and exhausted, but I couldn't see a way to change anything. I coped by telling myself "this is everyone's dream life" and then focusing on the next big event.

But I couldn't keep this pace up forever. As I was driving to an event on Christmas Eve in 2014, my smartphone sat dinging and buzzing in my lap with notification after notification. Glancing at it, I could see texts, emails, and social media messages pouring in at a rapid rate...on Christmas Eve! Each ding was something I needed to do. Something to say "yes" to, something to take care of, something to attend, something to respond to... I had to pull the car over on the side of the road as I began to have a legitimate panic attack. I opened the car door for fresh air and began hyperventilating. My fingers and lips began to tingle with the lack of oxygen and I felt terrified as I felt myself losing control over my own body.

Eventually, I began to breathe more easily and continued my drive to the party, crying and shaking from the ordeal. I later referred to this episode as "Inbox Overload" and it was only the beginning of me realizing that I was cramming too much into my daily life.

Later that year I experienced debilitating pain in my back that no one could explain or fix. I was given pain pills and shots directly into my back from the chiropractor. When I left my job to relocate to a new city, I had a "Going Away" party but I was confined to the couch the entire time. Friends bent down to say farewell and give me an awkward hug, as I couldn't move my neck or back. Soon after this point, I started learning how to say "No" to invitations. I was finally beginning to apply intentionality to the pacing of my life.

A massive 16-wheeler moving truck was needed to move all of our belongings across the country. Nothing was decluttered. Instead, movers came in and wrapped every single item. My absurd amount of clothes were zipped up into packaging by the dozens. The new apartment's garage where these items would be unloaded was utterly packed with boxes—we just had little trails carved through this makeshift storage unit to try and find our belongings. In my new city, I began experiencing unexplainable hives. In retrospect, it is easy to see that I was stressed and overwhelmed by the volume of stuff and my body was physically trying to slow me down to notice.

To make a long story short, I was very unhappy in my marriage. Without going into detail, at least a portion of the reason for my unhappiness was this focus on appearances and accumulation. Most of our time together was wasted watching TV. The "real me" felt trapped beneath my fancy clothes and hived skin. I wanted to get outside and explore. I wanted to travel. I wanted to create art, make music, and write stories. But I was constantly "too busy," and I wasn't sure why. In the end, we divorced.

I left with my insane amount of shoes and clothes, and bought an entire apartment's worth of new furniture from IKEA for my new 1,200-square foot space. At least this time, I did surround myself with light, airy furniture and artwork that I loved. But I still had a large U-Haul worth of stuff.

Eventually, I settled down with my soulmate. He moved in and hardly owned a thing: two surfboards, five t-shirts, two board shorts, two pairs of shoes, a few guitars and a stereo speaker. I'm not exaggerating—I think that was all he owned! He had spent the previous five years traveling the world as a surfing nomad—with only a backpack and a surfboard. He was full of life and stories and he valued his freedom and flexibility. I wanted that so badly! His good habits and philosophies began to rub off on me, slowly but surely.

Once again, I packed up my things to make a huge move across the country—now as a newlywed. Before packing, I ended up reading Marie Kondo's "The Life-Changing Magic of Tidying Up." Simply reading this book did not make me a minimalist. I was still far from it. But it was the very first inkling of what I needed to do to begin freeing myself. I questioned if things "sparked joy" and decluttered my items for the very first time in my life. It felt like I had gottten rid of a lot, and yet we still managed to fill up an entire trailer and my SUV. Amazingly, that was not enough! I still had so much stuff that we ended up having to rent a U-Haul truck as well—and even with that, we had to literally leave items on the sidewalk, as I could not cram them in. I still owned too much stuff.

Our new apartment was only 750-square feet with the world's tiniest closets. Immediately, I had to declutter further as my items simply would not fit into this space. Somehow, I still managed to pack as much as I could into the closets and under beds. My husband helpfully built more shelving in the laundry space, bathroom and kitchen, in an effort to find more storage. I felt okay with this…until we had our first child.

Having a baby was the catalyst for me to become a true minimalist. For the first year of her life, I became increasingly overwhelmed with my duties of being a housewife while keeping this destructive little human alive. The perfectionist in me kept me cleaning on a perpetual loop. I felt like I was not doing a good job in my new role unless my house was clean and tidy. And yet I was so torn because what I *really* wanted to be doing was spending time with my baby. It became apparent to me just how fleeting time was now that I had a child. She was growing by leaps and bounds every time I blinked! I could feel the precious time slipping from my fingers as I bent over to pick up more toys off the floor and scrubbed more dishes.

At the same time, I jealously watched my handsome husband return from an hour of surfing. He glowed with health and passion. His cup was still full and his interests were still fulfilled. Meanwhile, I craved time to exercise to lose my "baby weight." I craved time to read a book. I craved time to create art, play oboe and write. It felt unfair that I had to continually clean the house and change the diapers. My cup was very, very empty.

At my husband's continual but gentle urging, the philosophy around minimalism slowly began to sink in. At its most basic level: The less I had to clean, the more time I would have. I stumbled upon some very helpful podcasts on the subject and began drinking the information in. I dug deeper into books about minimalism, began shifting my mindset, and caught the decluttering fever—I finally started throwing things away!

It did not happen overnight. It took three years of constantly evaluating my items, asking deeper and deeper questions, uncovering all sorts of things about myself that I hadn't realized before, steadily decluttering and changing my shopping habits, until I finally felt the massive sigh of relief when I walked into my peaceful home and discovered I had ample time to play with my children and tackle creative pursuits.

We now have only two adult plates and two child plates. Putting everything else away in a cabinet reserved for the rare guest or dinner party, we reduced our family dinnerware to just the essentials and I've never had to run the dishwasher again. We simply rinse our plate after dinner and the kitchen remains clean. I cut our clothing down to capsule wardrobes, so there is no longer a full couch of laundry to tackle as a day-long project. Instead, the loads are small and instantly rolled into our few drawers which allows me to see every article of clothing at a glance. I got rid of furniture that I identified as clutter magnets, such as the office desk. Instead, I sit at our one small dining table with my laptop. The toys were distilled into a few baskets and are easy to pick up. We have no TV and our backyard is set up in a way that encourages all of us to play outdoors. When the kids are outside all day long, there is nothing to really clean up indoors!

But after all that, Christmas still remained a challenge. My child's first Christmas was absolutely absurd. I think "Santa" brought every gift a little girl needs for the first five years of her life...in one year. My excitement over finally "playing Santa" and creating "the magic" for a child of my own got way out of hand, and I did not set any limits or budget. Of course, as a one-year-old, she'll never remember that "magical" first Christmas with a living room overflowing with toys—including a miniature car, a three-story dollhouse, an antique wicker pram, and a rocking horse. I now know that simply giving her a stick, a ball, and a box would have been plenty for a one-year-old.

Right after that abundant Christmas I began making massive changes to my mindset towards "things." There were bigger and bigger purges and I purchased less and less. Every Christmas since has gotten smaller and simpler as I continue to whittle it down and take more control over what enters my home, even as my family has continued to grow.

As I talked with other moms about simplifying and intentionality, I noticed that the same questions kept arising: "How do you prepare a child for a smaller Christmas?" "How do I ask my family to buy less things?" "How do you find time to do all those wonderful things with your children?" "I heard you were saving money to retire early—how are you still saving during Christmas?"

It finally occurred to me that minimalism during the holidays can prove challenging even to already well-practiced minimalists. Even minimalists still get recommendations from Amazon and have to navigate event invitations as the busy season ramps up. It is my hope that this book will help guide anyone to have a simpler, more intentional Christmas holiday. The holidays take extra focus and I hope that this book gives you the tips and tools needed to make a mindset shift that sets you up for a peaceful and joyful season.

2

THE ORIGINS OF A CONSUMERIST HOLIDAY

Before we get into the more practical, actionable tips on how to slow down this season, I think it's helpful to examine why we have so many traditions urging us to spend money and stay busy. Understanding where this all stems from can help you shift your mindset as you shed a lifetime of cultural programming.

The vast majority of our Christmas traditions are "brand new" marketing schemes, when you consider the history of the holidays. Understanding this can help you decide to opt-out of consumerist-driven activities and objects, and help you whittle it down to the traditions that bring you and your family joy.

THE HISTORY OF AMERICA'S SANTA

The origins of the Christmas holiday on December 25th can arguably be traced back to pagan traditions—the Germanic Yule and the lawless, drunken Roman Saturnalia. These traditions included festivities, a form of fruitcake, mistletoe, caroling and wreaths. After solstice, the darkest night of the year, the renewal of light and the coming of the new year was celebrated in the later Roman Empire at the Dies Natalis of Sol Invictus, the "Birthday of the Unconquerable Sun," on December 25th. Later, early Christian missionaries under the rule of Constantine adopted this date to mark the birth of Jesus, who received gifts of frankincense, myrrh and gold, despite historical evidence showing he was likely born in the springtime.

Around 280 A.D. in what is now modern-day Turkey, St. Nicholas was born—a monk who became the source of legends, known for giving away all of his inherited wealth to the poor and sick as he traveled the countryside.

Centuries upon centuries went by before the next important moment in the story of modern-day Christmas.

St. Nicholas first entered American popular culture in 1773 and 1774 when a New York newspaper reported that groups of Dutch families had gathered to honor the anniversary of his death. Saint Nicholas/Sint Nikolaas/Sinter Klaas would eventually morph into "Santa Claus" in this newspaper report. In 1804, a member of the New York Historical Society distributed woodcuts of St. Nicholas, which included a background of now-familiar images of stockings filled with toys and fruit hung over the fireplace. In 1809, Washington Irving popularized the Sinter Klaas stories when he referred to St. Nicholas in his book "A History of New York" as the patron saint of New York.

In 1820, stores began to advertise Christmas shopping —particularly centering gift-giving around children. By the

1840s newspapers were creating separate sections for these holiday advertisements, often with images of the newly-popular Santa Claus.

In 1823, Clement Clarke Moore, an Episcopal minister, wrote a long Christmas poem for his three daughters titled "An Account of a Visit from St. Nicholas." You probably recognize this as "Twas The Night Before Christmas." He was hesitant to publish his poem due to the "frivolous nature" of its subject, but is now largely responsible for our modern image of Santa Claus as a "right jolly old elf" with a portly figure and the magical ability to ascend a chimney.

In 1841, a Philadelphia shop offered a life-size Santa Claus model and thousands of children came to visit. Other stores quickly caught on to the rage and began to lure children along with their parents to visit and peek at a "live" Santa Claus. In 1863, political cartoonist Thomas Nast illustrated two images, published in *Harper's Weekly* magazine, which cemented the nation's obsession with the portly elf. The first drawing shows Santa distributing presents in a Union Army camp, in a sleigh being pulled by reindeer. Santa is depicted giving allegiance in the Civil War, by wearing a jacket patterned with stars and pants colored in stripes.

Nast's second illustration features Santa in the periphery of a drawing flying in his sleigh, as well as showing him going down a chimney. Nast's images drew on Moore's poem to create the first Santa that matches our modern-day image of Santa Claus. His cartoons depict Santa as rotund and cheerful. His depictions of Santa show that he has a full, white beard and holds a sack full of toys for lucky children. His Santa has a bright red suit trimmed with white fur, a pointed cap with fur around its perimeter and a furry tassel on top. Not only did Nast assign Santa his suit, but he also gave him his North Pole workshop, elves and his wife, Mrs. Claus.

In the early 1890s, The Salvation Army began dressing up unemployed men in Santa Claus suits and sending them into the streets of New York to solicit donations. These bell-ringing Santas are still poised on America's street corners and store entrances to this day.

While America was developing its story of Santa Claus, similar St. Nicholas-inspired gift-givers were being celebrated as Christmas traditions and myths around the world, such as Christkind and Kris Kringle, who delivered presents to well-behaved Swiss and German children. Christkind (meaning "Christ child") is an angel-like figure that accompanies St. Nicholas on his holiday missions. There is also the Germanic Frau Holle, who treats women during Solstice. A jolly elf in Scandinavia named Jultomten delivers gifts in a sleigh drawn by goats. English legend is that "Father Christmas" visits each home on Christmas Eve to fill children's stockings with holiday treats. In France, it is Père Noël who is responsible for filling the shoes of French children. In Russia, it is believed that an elderly woman named Baboushka purposely gave the wise men wrong directions to Bethlehem so that they couldn't find Jesus. Feeling remorseful, Babouschka visits Russian children on January 5th and leaves gifts at their bedsides in the hopes that one of them is the baby Jesus and she will be forgiven. In Italy, a similar story exists about a woman called La Befana, a kindly witch who rides a broomstick down the chimneys of Italian homes to deliver toys into the stockings of lucky children on the "Good List."

In an increasingly global society, it is easy to see how these abundant gift-giving stories contributed to the overarching story of Santa Claus. Going forward, I think you'll be able to recognize the pattern of marketing and big business that continues to exploit this charming story.

In 1924, the Macy's Thanksgiving Day Parade began and featured a Macy's Santa both in the parade and in its New York City mall, where children lined up to take photos in Santa's lap. Coca-Cola also began including Santa in its advertising in the 1920s. Their Santa was strict looking, in the style of Thomas Nast.

In 1931, Coca-Cola hired an advertising agency to change the look of Santa, and he became the more wholesome version we see today. The massive soda company would then add a sprite (an elf) called "Sprite-Boy" as Santa's assistant for two decades of advertising in the 1940s and 1950s before launching their "Sprite" product in the 1960s.

In 1934, the Christmas song "Santa Claus is Coming to Town" immortalized the idea of a "Good List" and a "Naughty List" and parents often invoke these lists as a way to ensure their children are on their best behavior. Stores are happy and ready to help these parents reward good behaving children.

Over a hundred years after his eight counterparts were invented, the book "Rudolph The Red-Nosed Reindeer" was penned in 1939 by Robert L. May, a copywriter at the Montgomery Ward department store. "The most famous reindeer of all" proved to be quite popular and Montgomery Ward sold almost two and a half million copies of the story in 1939. When it was reissued in 1946, the book sold over three and half million copies. In 1949, one of May's friends, Johnny Marks, wrote a short song based on Rudolph's story. It was recorded by Gene Autry and sold over two million copies. The story would later become a globally celebrated movie narrated by Burl Ives in 1964.

In 1950, Gene Autry recorded the popular song "Frosty the Snowman" to follow the success of his Rudolph hit the year before. Like "Rudolph," "Frosty" was subsequently adapted to other media including a popular television special, *Frosty the Snowman*. The ancillary rights to *Frosty* are owned by Warner Bros., and merchandising of the character is generally licensed in tandem with that special's current owners, DreamWorks Classics. While details such as this may not mean much to most people, I share this to drive home the point that large corporations are behind much of the quaint imagery we include in our holiday traditions.

In 2005, the children's picture book with an accompanying toy elf called "The Elf on the Shelf: A Christmas Tradition" was released by Carol Aebersold and her daughter Chanda Bell. The premise of the story was that a little elf was sent from the North Pole to watch over children. At night, the elf would return to Santa to tell him about the children's behavior and return home to take up a new position in the house. Chippy, The Elf on the Shelf, joined the Macy's Day Parade as a massive balloon in 2012, cementing himself as a holiday staple. A 2016 article stated that revenue from the family-owned business has increased at an average annual rate of 150%. The company's value increased to almost $85 million in 2015.

The Elf on the Shelf phenomenon is still fairly new and reveals that we are *still* crafting the story around Santa Claus. The marketing and Big Business that comes with it is still developing at a rapid rate and we are continually adopting these stories as a part of our mainstream culture.

THE BIG BUSINESS OF A CONSUMERIST CHRISTMAS

According to a study performed by the National Retail Federation, Americans were projected to spend more money on gifts in 2018 than they did at any other time. According to a Gallup study, American adults were projected to spend approximately $920 on gifts per person, up from $885 per person in the previous year, with total holiday spending exceeding $1 trillion nationwide. According to this study, the breakdown on gift buying in 2018 was:

- 33% expected to spend at least $1000 on gifts.
- 22% expected to spend between $500 and $999.
- 29% expected gift spending to be between $100 and $499.
- 3% planned to spend less than $100.
- 8% planned to spend no money.
- 5% were unsure.

So you can see from the figures that the vast majority are spending a shocking number on gifts each year. Media is saturated with advertisements and influencers. It is a well-oiled machine crafted to induce impulse-buying and overspending.

Americans have been spending more on holiday gifts every year since 2008 (except for 2012), much of that increasingly being purchased online. According to a study released by Mastercard, e-commerce sales in 2019 made up 14.6% of total retail and rose 18.8% from the 2018 period, from November 1 through Christmas Eve, with 24.5% of all holiday season shopping happening on "Cyber Monday" (the Monday after Thanksgiving).

Amazon said billions of items were ordered worldwide in 2019, and the number of products delivered with free one-day and same-day shipping nearly quadrupled in the U.S. The online retail giant called the holiday season "record-breaking," and it said it sold more than half a billion items in its newly launched brick-and-mortar stores.

The best-selling items on Amazon.com for the 2019 holiday season included the company's Echo Dot, Fire TV Stick with Alexa Voice Remote and Echo Show—all of which are items that listen to your every whim and desire in the background of your home. While their marketed intention is to act as helpful voice-activated devices (i.e. "Alexa, play a song." "Alexa, add milk to the grocery list."), these devices can then collect that data and theoretically have even more highly targeted advertisements or "recommendations" for you the next time you log in to purchase an item. Indeed, you can order on impulse by speaking to the device the moment a thought occurs to you ("Alexa, order a trampoline"). It's shocking to consider that the best-selling Christmas item is a device that will enable us to spend even more money, even more thoughtlessly.

Even with online sales reporting exponential growth, the brick-and-mortar retail growth is still going strong. Black Friday (the day following Thanksgiving) in 2019 was a record-setting day for sales. Even though the rest of the world does not celebrate the U.S. Thanksgiving holiday, the holiday shopping tradition has been adopted in other countries and Black Friday sales hit $20 billion globally.

On Thanksgiving Day itself—a time when families should ideally be joined around a table together eating comfort foods, followed by sitting around in a blissful food coma afterward—sales went up as well, passing $4.4 billion. After expressing thanks and gratitude for all that they have, they are running out to buy all that they *don't* have.

It's all a bit sickening, is it not?

My hope is that by reading this quick history lesson and seeing these very real, and very shocking numbers, you will understand what a relatively new phenomenon this Christmas-hullabaloo truly is.

The traditions embedded in the winter holidays go as far back as the Greeks and Romans. Religion has tacked on another level of importance and reverence. Then a combination of children's stories and savvy marketing has swept us up in a bevy of traditions and myths that urge us to spend money. We now simply expect to trade our hard-earned money for gifts and events. Many people spend their entire year budgeting and preparing for the lump sum of cash (and even debt) that will suddenly be needed to participate in society's "happiest time of the year."

Marketing, advertising, technology and Big Data understand our psychology and habits better than we know ourselves. The reduction of "friction" with slick technology is funneling away our money faster than we can produce it, and the accumulation of new items is then sucking away our time and our sanity.

With less money and less time we experience an increased level of stress.

So put these dates and numbers in perspective whenever you feel that urge to spend. I'm not telling you to not participate in Christmas or not to partake in these traditions, but remembering it's a relatively new, largely artificial concept might help you to scale back. This awareness can be a helpful tool.

The modern-day American Santa Claus is still not even 200 years old. Rudolph and Frosty are about 70 years old and The Elf on the Shelf is 15 years old. Even the Amazon Prime membership program—through which the vast majority of online holiday shopping currently takes place—is only 15 years old. While there is certainly magic that can be created around these mythical stories for children, it cannot be denied that the root of all this is Big Business.

You don't have to be a part of that money-generating machine. It can stop with you. You can determine how much value the "story" of Christmas should have in your household. You can decide where you want to spend your time.

You can adopt a minimalist lifestyle at any time of the year, but if there were ever a season to get laser-focused on shutting out the cultural clamor for "more," it would be during the holidays.

3

DECLUTTERING IN ADVANCE

Now that you feel ill from the sheer ridiculousness of it all, it's time to take action!

In an effort to find peace within your own home during the busy holidays, I find that the best way to begin preparing for this season is to start with your personal environment. Decluttering not only releases any anxiety you may be feeling in the moment, but it will also help you make room (both in space and in time) for the things that really matter to you throughout the entire season.

Decide right now that you will not let *stuff* steal from you any longer. Managing and cleaning your stuff can easily steal away your time if the volume of stuff has slowly crept up on you. Or it may have become such a burden that you are no longer able to manage or clean it.

Time is the most valuable asset we have. It is irreplaceable and finite. Our life is created by a collection of moments. Don't let your belongings steal away your life's precious moments and potential. By exercising intentionality, you can distill your belongings down to the things your family truly loves, needs and uses. Cut away the excess and you'll see how much time you can gain by not constantly cleaning up and feeling overwhelmed by the large household projects. I highly recommend pursuing minimalism for your entire home and in all aspects of your life. There are several amazing books already published on the topic of minimalism and decluttering your entire home. However, now (right before the holidays) is probably not the time to tackle an enormous lifestyle change. I am not recommending you try to declutter your entire home, nor do I think it's something that most people can achieve in a weekend, month or even a year. Truly cutting your home down to the essentials and getting every family member on board is something that takes a lot of discipline and time. I recommend you look into this on a deeper level after the New Year.

Right now, you're simply looking at decluttering the main areas of your life that are affected by the holidays. Even if you are already a minimalist, it's worth giving these areas fresh attention, as everyone eventually accumulates more items over time.

The areas I encourage you to focus on are:
- Children's Rooms
- Kitchen
- Winter Wardrobes
- Living Room

CHILDREN'S ROOMS

The areas where your children's toys accumulate are the first spots to tackle and the most important. If you cannot get around to decluttering the next three areas on the list, make sure you have at least checked off this particular task.

Even if you have asked family members not to send gifts, and even if you have instilled the 4-Gift Rule (details in Chapter 8), we live in a culture that celebrates Christmas gift-giving. New items *will* make their way into your home, despite even your best efforts to slow it down.

The best way to mitigate stress and overwhelm down the road is to go ahead and make room for these items. Take a moment to look around your children's bedrooms and/or playrooms and locate the items your children have not played with very much over the past year or more. Set up a box for donations, another for trash, another for keepsakes, and a pile for "keepers" that will remain in the room in a new, more organized way.

The first step is the easiest one to tackle: Locate any broken toys or incomplete sets and simply throw them in the trash!

While you are surveying the room, notice when you rationalize certain toys simply because *you* like them. You may notice your own resistance to declutter the items you purchased yourself, or the items that are aesthetically pleasing and match the room's decor. Has your child ever shown any interest in these items? Really? Are you holding onto them simply because you are attached to them emotionally or because of sunk-cost-bias? If the item doesn't serve your children, it should not remain in the room. This clutter adds to their mental overwhelm and adds more items for you to later clean up.

Notice when you rationalize certain toys simply because they were a gift. Just because an aunt or grandmother gave a toy to your children years ago, does not mean these toys have to stick around forever. If you realize that the majority of excess toys are in the room because they were gifts, don't fall into the trap of a negative mindset where you start grumbling about them. Don't resent people for their generosity. Mentally thank them for their contributions that once created smiles, and then bag the toys up for donations or trash. It is a blessing and a privilege to have people who care about your children and want to add to their joy or "help you out" by "financially contributing." It is not their fault if they do not realize how their gifts are now contributing to excess. Take a deep breath, practice gratitude, and practice how you might gently approach these gift-givers about future offerings (see Chapter 8).

Donate gently-used items and recycle when you can. This is another great teaching moment as a parent. Discuss with your children what it means to donate and include them in the process of dropping the toys off at a charitable center. Explain to them how they can offer a second-life to their toys by passing them to another child who may not be as blessed as they are with such abundance. 'Tis the season of giving, after all, and this is a great way to both teach this lesson and add more peace to your own lives as well.

It is up to you whether you want to include your child in this decluttering process or not. It really depends on their age and their maturity. If they are under 3 or 4, it is likely easiest to do this yourself, with no input from the child. They really won't notice after their space has been tidied. But if they see you throwing toys out, they'll likely protest, have a tantrum, and start pulling items out of the boxes.

If they are a few years older, you may want to do a hybrid approach—perhaps doing an initial sweep first and bagging up the more obvious things, and then ask them to help you sort through what is left in the room and do a deeper sweep together. At this age, I would recommend avoiding any future rage by letting them look into your bags and give them the opportunity to pull out any items they disagree with. Prepare yourself to accept that their decisions will be different from yours. Try focusing on the long-term picture: Teaching your child good decluttering habits.

Any older, then you really should include them in the entire process, so that they don't resent future efforts of minimalism and lash out by hoarding, afraid that you'll take their precious items away. This is a great teaching moment for you as a parent, to help walk them through the entire process of evaluating whether something is trash, or something they've grown out of and could donate to someone in need.

Another strategy to consider is bribes. Yes, bribes. I have not tried this strategy out myself, but other mothers have shared with me their stories of successful incentives. For a specific example, try removing all of the toys from the room except a few obvious keepers. Give your child $20 and tell them that for every toy they decide to retrieve from outside of the room, it will cost them $1. They can squander any remaining money on sweets if they want. Assigning value and setting the parameters of how many items are allowed to remain will get them to assess their toys on a deeper level.

Give each child one box to keep sentimental items in. You should have one for yourself, too. Sometimes there's a doll-baby too precious to throw out (just yet). Or maybe it's the miniature lace socks they wore home from the hospital, and you decide you want to keep that in your own sentimental box. The key thing to remember is that the box is the limit. No extra boxes can be added. The lid has to be able to shut on it. If anybody's box gets too full, then it's time to declutter the box and whittle it down to the sentimental items that mean the most. This will be an ongoing process for everyone in the family till the end of time. Starting the kids now with a "safe space" to stow their treasures is a great way to teach them to put a limit on the things they label as sentimental and emotional.

Now that you've pared the toys down to the items that they truly love and play with (hopefully you have been able to cut it down roughly 25-50%), there will be much more space left in the room to allow any new Christmas items to comfortably find a spot on the shelf or in the toy box. You'll find Christmas Day much less stressful when you know that the new items have a space waiting for them.

KITCHEN

If you can find the time, I highly recommend you tackle the kitchen next for a quick decluttering sweep. A helpful trick for tidying any room is to first "set the intent." Close your eyes and imagine what an ideal version of your kitchen would look like and how it would function. *What is the intent of this room?* And as the holidays approach, narrow the focus of this question even further: *What is the intent of this room for Christmas?*

You see, the kitchen may shift its role a little bit during the holidays. To give a personal example, the main focus for my kitchen during the majority of the year is the coffee station, the fruit bowls, and ample countertop space with organized herbs for cooking dinners. But during the holiday season, sugar admittedly takes center stage. I love setting up a hot cocoa bar, complete with mini marshmallows in an apothecary candy jar, packets of powder, stir sticks, and my collection of peppermint-swirled hot cocoa mugs. When I am hosting, I love to also have a wassail (mulled apple cider) station set up, complete with appropriate glasses and port. And all season long, I love to bake sweets, so my baking supplies need to be organized for action.

So, this means I need to pull out all of my baking supplies, declutter, take inventory and reorganize them. This way I know exactly how many bags of brown sugar I've accumulated, or how little flour I have left in the pantry. I locate my rolling pin and my tin cookie cutters. I know if I still have leftover red and green sprinkles, or if I have enough vanilla extract and cinnamon on hand. I create space on an easily accessible shelf to house all of the baking supplies that otherwise might be stowed in a less important space during the rest of the year.

This helps reduce stress during the actual baking process (especially with the added chaos of managing children playing with flour and dough!) and also reduces the amount I spend at the grocery store, since I know exactly what I already have on hand at home, and which items need to be restocked.

The intent of your kitchen may be completely different from mine. So take a moment to really sit with that and decide how you need your kitchen to best function over the Christmas period.

You do not need to do a deep decluttering of your kitchen. Don't tackle every single drawer and cabinet. That is a huge project that should probably be left for sometime in the New Year. Right now, I would focus on making sure your countertops are as clear as possible and that any "stations" for holiday-related reasons are set up in a way that makes the most sense for your home. (Sometimes these stations may make more sense outside of the kitchen, perhaps on a bar cart or a small table in the living room, dining room, or other entertaining space).

WINTER WARDROBES

Another helpful spot to declutter before the holidays arrive is your family's winter wardrobe.

First, let's start with your own wardrobe. Open your closet and pull out everything you would possibly wear in the wintertime: sweaters, long sleeve shirts, leggings, pants, hats, gloves, boot socks, scarves, coats, and any dresses or outfits that would make sense to wear to a Christmas party.

I love the Marie Kondo "Konmarie Method" of tossing everything into a pile on the bed. The visual impact of the sheer amount of stuff you own is enough to spur most people into more discerning declutterers. Remember, you're not doing your entire wardrobe—just your winter wardrobe. You can replicate this exercise to include everything you own another day.

Make a quick pass through this pile and sort things into Keep, Trash, or Donate piles. Then, go through your Keep pile and quickly try on every single item and give an honest look in the mirror. If the item no longer fits you or is obviously outdated, reconsider it and either add it to the Donate pile or hang it up in the very back of your closet to be dealt with when you have the time to do a complete wardrobe decluttering project later in the New Year (this is supposed to be a fairly quick decluttering exercise—an hour tops!)

By trying the items on, you will hopefully hone in on the outfits that make you *feel* the best. You are doing the "hard" work of groaning in the mirror *now*, rather than later. This way, when it is the night of a big Christmas party, you don't waste hours trying on things and feeling bad about yourself when the tenth outfit doesn't fit well. If you set yourself up for ease and joy in advance, when the big party arrives, you can simply reach in and locate the dress that makes you feel fantastic and know in advance that it does indeed still fit you. Getting dressed will feel stress-free and take very little time, and you'll continue feeling joyful for the entire evening.

Once you've completed sorting your winter wardrobe, you can now put the items in the Keep pile back into your closet and drawers in a forefront position. Push the spring and summer things further to the back, so that your winter items are all gathered together in the most easy-to-see location.

Similar to organizing baking supplies so that you know your current inventory, you'll now know precisely how many winter clothing items you own. Most likely you won't need to go out and purchase anything else. But you might realize that every single pair of jeans just went into the Donate pile, and it is now time to budget getting one or two new pairs in a size that fits.

If you do end up going shopping, I highly recommend you consider creating a "capsule wardrobe" of sorts. You don't have to go out and complete this project right now, in the midst of holiday prep, but begin giving it some thought so that anything you purchase new may be fairly neutral in color, and of a classic design.

A capsule wardrobe does not have to have a specific number or limit to the amount of pieces, though many people find it helpful to create limits for themselves. I like to think of a capsule wardrobe more like a closet full of your favorite things that all happen to mix and match well. Capsule wardrobes work best with timeless style, rather than something super trendy. Take a look at your closet and locate your all-time favorite pieces. Why are they your favorite? How can you replicate that and expand on it?

How to create a capsule wardrobe

To give a personal example, I used to have very fashionable, trendy pieces in every style, color and print. My closet was PACKED and yet I never found anything I wanted to wear. I trapped myself in a cycle of "Well I've worn that already and I don't want anyone to see me in it again since it is so memorable," and so I went out and bought something new to wear. When I finally started searching for my personal style to create a capsule wardrobe, I discerned that my favorite pieces were all some variation of white. And if the white items were tops, I only wanted to pair them with jeans or black leggings.

Suddenly, my new "uniform" was very easy to whittle down: Anything white, cream, bone or ivory stayed. I kept my favorite denim and black pieces. I hauled out an embarrassing amount of bright colors and loud prints to donate. Now, when I go shopping, I have automatic "blinders" on to shield me from today's current trends. Almost nothing on the racks fits into my classic capsule wardrobe, and I now feel immune to the urge to even look at those bright floral prints. If it doesn't fit my guideline, it won't disturb my peaceful closet.

The added bonus of a capsule wardrobe is the elimination of "decision fatigue." I had no idea that I suffered from it until I created my capsule wardrobe and felt the weight suddenly lift off of me! I no longer waste any time hemming and hawing over what to wear. I don't need to try on three outfits before I land on something I love. I don't need to plan outfits out in advance. I don't have to decide if a certain color is appropriate for the season. I just reach in, grab something white, and open a drawer to grab something denim. Whalaa! Every single piece is one I love, so I could reach into my closet blindfolded and be assured that I would love whatever it is I pulled out.

After the holidays, I really encourage you to start chiseling away until you discover your specific timeless style, and cut this energy-sucking decision making out of your life for good!

Now that you have accomplished setting yourself up for a more peaceful season of getting dressed for cold weather and special events, it's time to replicate that same process for your children and spouse (grown children and adults make their own decluttering decisions, of course!). What good is it to peacefully get dressed for a party, only to still stress yourself out trying to wrangle small children into stockings and scarves and locating missing mittens and boots?

Sort through the miniature clothes and figure out what sizes your children are currently in and only get those items out. Clear out a drawer just for winter items or find some way to best organize their seasonal outfits so that your family functions more smoothly for the next few months. If you know there is a dressy event coming up, go ahead and make sure dress-shirts are ironed for any males in your household. The goal is for your family to be able to get dressed thirty minutes before time to leave and everyone knows where their items are and no extra work is required on anyone's part—especially yours. Even if you don't plan to attend any formal events during the holiday season, editing the household's clothes will help keep rooms looking tidy, laundry from getting bogged down, and all members of the family more independent as they can easily locate their winter items. Again, you're doing the "hard" work now so that you don't have to do it during the days that you would prefer to be exuding joy.

LIVING AREA

Lastly, give your main living area or den a once-over. There's no need to do any major work here, but just tidy the space up and rearrange, if necessary, so that it makes the most sense to accommodate your family and any Christmas decorations you plan to put up.

The Christmas tree, should you choose to have one, is usually the focal point and is like adding another piece of furniture to the room. It is likely that once you've brought in a tree, certain pieces of furniture will need to be moved— perhaps even to a different room. Spend a few minutes or a few days thinking about the best set-up for this temporary room arrangement. Prep whatever you can before you get out boxes of decorations. If you plan to have your family do the decorating together, then do a little prep work to make that event as peaceful and easy as possible.

Again, "setting the intent" is a helpful process here. Does your family like watching Christmas movies like a marathon event leading to the big day? Then make sure the couch, armchairs, tv, or projector are set up in the coziest and most logical way. Does your family prefer to break out the Christmas puzzles and work on those together? Then make sure you have a dedicated table set up in a nook. Does your family enjoy reading Christmas books together? Then create a special basket or shelf to house your collection of Christmas books and set it next to the biggest armchair with a lamp nearby. Does your family like to do tons of seasonal arts and crafts and make homemade gifts? Then perhaps you should shift your focus to the dining table area or office desk area and set up a temporary station of sorts nearby with the craft supplies accessible.

The living area is often the most decorated room of the home and if you can clearly set the intent of the room, it will feel less cluttered once you introduce decorations. This area is the gathering spot for everyone in your family, and sets the tone for your Christmas experience. It may need the least amount of decluttering work, but it may prove to be the most important space for coziness and peace this season.

DON'T DECLUTTER EVERYTHING

Save a full decluttering of your home for *after* the holidays. You only need to address the main areas that will be in use for this season. During the calmer months of February and

March you'll find the time and energy to deep-dive into minimalism and do a full decluttering of your home. Don't let the anticipation of that overwhelm you. The decluttering process never actually ends, though it will get quicker and easier. This will be a lifestyle change that takes constant diligence, as items still manage to creep into the tidiest of homes. As you tackle the psychological reasons you both accumulate and hold onto items, it will become easier. For me, that took several years of studying and practicing minimalism as a process and a mindset. Remember that you are only decluttering the spaces most relevant to this season, so that your household functions more smoothly and you can set the stage for a calm Christmas.

4

INTENTIONALITY

The key word for preparing a Minimalist Christmas is *intentionality*. Every moment you experience, every dollar you spend, every item you decide to introduce into your world should be done in the most intentional way—on purpose, consciously, deliberately.

In this chapter, we'll explore how you can apply intentionality in your decorating and managing your time throughout the holidays.

SIMPLIFYING DECORATING

With your main spaces decluttered, it's time to move on to intentional decorating. I won't tell you how to decorate your space, aesthetically. That is totally up to you. Everyone's personal style, collections, and traditions are different. A Minimalist Christmas does not mean that your house will be all-white with a completely bare evergreen tree in the corner by your Swedish mid-mod furniture. While visions of clean, white spaces with ample negative space have become associated with minimalism, it is only one interpretation.

When becoming more minimal in your decorating, you can work with what you already own and with your own personal style, whether that's traditional, shabby chic, bohemian, or your own eclectic taste. In order to do that intentionally and more simply, we need to really dig into "The Ghost of Christmas Past" and determine what things were adding to our overwhelm in previous years. This probably means scaling back the amount of decorating you do.

So go ahead and pull out all of your boxes from previous Christmases. Fight the urge to follow your usual decorating routine. If you have children, try to get this task done before the actual "decorating day," so little hands don't start digging in and setting things out. Simply open the boxes and take a peek at what is inside each one and get an overall feel for the inventory you have to work with.

Are there any aspects you dread? Do you remember which aspects of the decorating were difficult to take down and pack up? Was there something you set out last year that got no attention or use?

Which items make you feel like a child again and make you brim with joy? Which items plaster a grin on your face and make you want to stand back in admiration?

Is there anything that looks like it's getting a bit too worn out? (For example: Are the red ribbons that were on last year's door wreath faded pink from the sun? Does the plaid throw blanket you draped on the corner of your couch have pilling with hopelessly tangled tassels? Is the faux greenery looking tattered and are the embedded bulbs not lighting up on one side?)

If an item is too worn out or broken, go ahead and toss it. I know it's hard to do because you probably remember how expensive it was when you bought it only a year or two ago. But sit with the emotions this brings because it will help guide you in future purchases (either to stop buying stuff like this altogether, or to be more discerning on the quality level you expect in the future).

Now examine the Christmas tree ornaments and ask these same questions. Identify the obvious trash and the obvious keepers. But for everything in between, start asking yourself why you are still keeping them. Were they gifts? Did you inherit them from your mother-in-law? Did you follow a trend or a certain color scheme one year? Did the kids make them and do they hold a lot of value to you? Were they the cheap ornaments you bought when you were a poor college kid decorating your first apartment? If they are not your absolute favorite ornaments, you don't need to offer them square footage in your house. Stop paying their rent. If they don't deserve the high honor of gracing your tree, then they certainly shouldn't still be squatting in your home. You can release them!

If they are still in decent shape, you can donate them to a local thrift shop or charity. If you are doing this process early enough in the season, you'll be getting rid of them during a time when others are actually looking for these items—so you'll feel less guilt and resistance in parting with them. Besides thrift shops and donation centers, you could list the items in your local 'Buy Nothing Group', Facebook Marketplace, Craigslist, or other popular online buy/sell/ trade sites. Do not box them back up and store them again! At this point, you should be left with the decorations you intend on setting out this year. It doesn't matter how much it is, you've put in some intentional thought about each piece. If decorating with your family is part of your holiday tradition, it should be a pretty smooth event this year, as no one will be sifting through the box to search for "the good stuff." Everything will be the good stuff.

Now, if you want to try going a level deeper, and you have a desire to "burn it all" and start from scratch to achieve an ultra-simple look, then try making your own decorations from the outdoors. That "Scandanavian" aesthetic is popular for a reason, after all. If you don't want to pack up boxes of decorations ever again, then simply start bringing nature indoors. Set up a live Christmas tree, string popcorn or cranberries to make a garland. Slice oranges and grapefruits and hang them with cinnamon and rosemary to fill your home with the scent of citrus and spices. Stick cloves in oranges and make a decorative topiary. Place a poinsettia plant in your home. Hang small pinecones in place of ornaments. When Christmas is all over, your entire decorative collection can be put on the compost pile and won't be adding to a landfill or take up storage space in your home. (*Download my free e-book for more details on creating this popular minimalist aesthetic! Visit the link located at the end of this book*).

Whichever direction you decide to go—whether a reduced and less chaotic version of Christmases past or your first attempt at having a completely natural and handmade Christmas—just be sure you're choosing the option that gives you the least amount of stress. Some people are overwhelmed by the cost and upkeep of store-bought decorations, while others are overwhelmed by the mere thought of DIY-ing their ornaments. Your gut should tell you in an instant which option will work best for you, but keep in mind that you can schedule in the crafting and it may give you a great sense of achievement. Whatever you're doing, just scale it back and remember *less is more*.

Edit to fit your family

Even after scaling my interior Christmas decorations back by a third one year, I still felt compelled to decorate the front of my house with lights. I let the pressure of my own former ideals push me to do something that was just not the right fit for my family. You see, my children were both very little, so it wasn't the family memory-making event my ideal-self imagined it to be. And my husband is very frugal and careful about using electricity. The grumbling and preaching from my spouse stripped away any idyllic magic and instead lighting the house up became a stressful and guilt-ridden experience. So even after all of the time I spent hanging these outdoor lights, I only turned them on maybe three times in one month. Then the lights remained hanging on the front of our house (turned off) until Valentine's Day! It was such a huge project that I procrastinated for a month and a half before finally making the time to crawl up on a ladder and take them down.

Next year, when I do my initial purge of unneeded decorations, I know that I will donate the entire box of outdoor Christmas lights. I doubt I will hang lights on the outside of our home again, as it just doesn't fit with our family. And that's okay! If I know it stresses my spouse out, then I will edit it out of future Christmases. I want everyone in our household to feel cozy, comfortable, and peaceful.

Getting rid of a few strands of lights from my routine not only will please my partner, but takes yet another item off my holiday checklist. For some families, decorating the house is likely a very fun tradition, but the key is that I recognize what is the right fit for *my* family.

What is the right fit for your family? Take a moment to pause and consider if anything you've been doing is feeling forced and more trouble than it's worth. Then edit it out.

BE INTENTIONAL WITH YOUR TIME

The next step is to carefully manage your family's time during the holiday season. I usually begin doing this in November, as many events happen the week after Thanksgiving, sometimes before you even enter December. Jot down a list of items you would ideally like to do together, and then begin mapping it out. Begin filling in your calendar with both "loose plans" and "hard plans." I'll explain how.

I keep a paper calendar hanging in the kitchen so that everyone in the family can see what is coming up. I find using a pencil on the paper calendar is the best place to start. Then once I am sure of which items I'll definitely be attending, they go into the digital calendar on my phone with alerts.

HARD PLANS

The "hard plans" are often the easiest to spot. Of course there is Christmas Day and Christmas Eve, and then there may be one-time events you want to attend. I often hop on a search engine or a social media calendar (such as Facebook Events) to find my area's holiday events. For example, the town's Annual Tree Lighting, photos with Santa (more on this later in the chapter), the Christmas Parade, the Nutcracker Ballet, the jazz band's and community orchestra's Christmas Concert, the local children's theatre performing 'The Grinch', the Tour of Historic Homes, the Holiday Arts & Crafts Maker's Market, etcetera. You are not planning to attend all of these types of events, but simply looking at your choices.

Once you've located all the events that have a specific date and time attached to them, you can fill out your calendar in pencil to get an idea of the spacing between them. If you notice several events happening one after another, then I would erase the ones that you are less likely to attend and pick your favorite from the bunch. You don't want to over-do it and exhaust everyone, including yourself. The remaining spaced-out events that you have chosen to keep are now your "hard plans." You could write the less-likely-to-attend events in tiny letters at the bottom of the date, just so that you remember that it is a possible *option* for that day. This is what I call a "loose plan" which I explain in further detail later in this chapter.

56

Many events are free—especially if you pack a lunch, or plan to eat dinner quickly before leaving for a free evening event and avoid the temptation of food trucks. However, about half of the events in my town that are possible "hard plans" are ticketed events. Do a quick search to find their prices. Jot these prices down on the calendar as well. For example, seeing "The Nutcracker" ballet is a tradition of ours that I absolutely love. However, the tickets are $30 for an adult ticket, $10 for children 3 and up. Since my husband is not a big fan of ballet, we agreed that this could be a tradition for just the children and me. Not every family tradition requires every single family member to participate. By respecting his non-interest and not pressuring him to attend, the tradition is not only more enjoyable, but also more affordable if it only costs $40 instead of $70. By planning in advance, I am able to discuss the budget with my spouse for any events that will cost money, so no one is left surprised and stressed over seemingly unnecessary bills. Communication and agreement with your partner about the budget takes away any guilt or anxiety that can often come with holiday purchases.

By looking at the ticket prices ahead of time, you can decide far in advance if an event looks worthwhile and whether it fits in your personal budget. This decision will be helpful later when you receive invitations from other friends who are planning to attend ticketed events. If a friend includes you in a text saying "Hey! We're heading to the holiday circus today at 3—anyone else wanna come?" you will feel more comfortable declining if you have already pre-made a decision to opt out of this particular event.

Saying No

Your life—especially during the holidays—can begin to feel very chaotic if you allow yourself to be pulled spontaneously into unplanned events. If you find yourself a person who says "Yes" to too many invitations or favors, then this section is for you.

This holiday, make an intentional effort to not automatically respond with a "Yes!" to an event, even if it sounds incredibly fun. Give yourself time to pause. Consider everything that is happening in your family's lives before and after that day. (If you have several things planned for an upcoming Saturday and Sunday, and a friend is inviting you to something on Friday afternoon, consider how this will affect everyone's energy level and enthusiasm for the things you had planned that weekend. Is it *too much?*)

You should also pause and consider:
- your overall calendar,
- the cost of the event,
- the time required traveling to the event (put the address in Google Maps to get an idea),
- the time of day and which meals will need to be purchased (or made at home and packed).

If any of these considerations begin to make you wince inside, then there's a good chance the answer should be a "No, thank you." Sometimes these types of things are absolutely worth it, but oftentimes, our gut instinct is telling us to *slow down*.

If you have a well laid-out calendar of events you aim to attend, stick to it and resist the urge to pack in every single thing you hear about. Don't let FOMO (fear of missing out) be the reason your family is broke, stressed and exhausted.

Saying "No" to people is extremely difficult for most people—especially people-pleasers. The holidays are a time when extra invitations seem to pour in as events and parties increase. You must have control over your time and your pacing if you are to have a less stressful, more intentional holiday, so learning to gracefully say "No" will release a lot of the pressure, guilt, resentment, anxiety and overwhelm that many people feel during this time of year.

Many studies have shown that we are hard-wired genetically to be social animals, as it was key to our survival as a species. Remember our evolution: You had to be accepted by the tribe of other cavemen in order to be allowed to sleep in the safe cave that night and to share the fire and food. Otherwise, you'd be left out in the elements with predators and likely not survive the night.

That hard-wiring has not left us, despite us living in a relatively safe environment with an abundance of food. So we still feel immense pressure to be accepted by "the tribe"—whether that is our own family, our circle of friends, or society at large. Understanding this point alone has helped me be able to decipher my own urges to participate in events or purchase items, and determine if my real motive is to fit into a group. If I have that realization, it's much easier to shake off that old caveman mentality and bring myself back into the modern world, where I can have much more control of my life.

Once you have detected that primal source of the urge to say "Yes," even when you know the answer should clearly be a "No," actually saying "No" can still feel incredibly uncomfortable because we naturally shun the feeling of letting another person down.

But you don't have to abruptly say "No" in order to decline an invitation or a purchase. You can gracefully bow out of a request by mastering some helpful language. Here are some phrases you can practice at home in advance of seeing friends and family, or when responding via messaging systems like social media, emails or text messages.

Eventually this language will feel more natural to you:

- Start with a "Thank you." Offering gratitude before declining is the simplest and easiest way to elegantly bow out of an invitation. For example, you might say, "Thanks for thinking of me! But I don't think I'll be able to attend" or "I appreciate your time, but no thank you."
- Say "Maybe" or "I'll definitely think about it!"
- Ask for more information, and if they do get back to you with the information, and your answer is still a "No" you can simply say "Thank you! I'll consider it" and often that can be the dead-end of the request.
- Say "I'm sorry, I can't right now." Most people have the urge to explain *why* they can't and start immediately spewing their justifications and detailing their busy life. You do not have to do that. It's much simpler to say this short phrase in a genuine,

apologetic tone. Keep it short and simple! (Note: It's okay to also do this even if you really *can*. If your personal reason is that you'd really rather just lie on the couch watching movies with your kids and never getting out of your pajamas, it's still okay to respond with a simple "I'm sorry, I can't today," or "Not today, thanks!" or, "I'm afraid I can't, but thanks for asking!" Don't guilt yourself and don't explain yourself.)

- Another way to dead-end a request in a gentle way is to say, "I'll get back to you." A good example of alluding to a busy life is to kindly respond, "I would love to! I just need to follow up on a few other things but will get back to you as soon as possible." When you never follow up, the requester will simply assume your life was too busy at the moment and will understand. It may feel a little flaky, especially if you are actually intentionally being the opposite of busy, but it's still better than not responding at all. It also can buy you some time to get the courage to confirm a few days later that you cannot join the event.

- Tell the truth. While I don't want anyone to feel compelled to explain themselves, you could let close friends know you are intentionally slowing down. Gently explain "We're trying to keep our calendar clearer this year so we don't get overwhelmed."
- One aspect of minimalism for many people is frugality. If your reason for wanting to decline is cost, then offer something else instead. For example, I often get asked to attend ticketed events (like going to the zoo or paying to go to a kids play zone) with other families so that our children can play together. Instead of simply declining, I often try to offer that they visit with us at our home and offer to make PB&Js instead, or I offer to meet up at a public park and suggest we bring

our own picnic lunches. If the family truly wants to get together purely to have the children play and for the grownups to chat, then they'll happily accept the playdate offer. If they would really prefer to be attending the ticketed event, it is now in their court to decline my counter-offer.

- Buy yourself time to answer by saying "Let me check..." For me, this is often my calendar that I genuinely do need to check. Examples of this tactic could be: "Let me check my with my manager," or "Let me check with my spouse," or "My schedule is packed right now, but I can let you know if I have an opening," or "My schedule is packed right now, but let me check my calendar and I can get back to you later."

- If you are genuinely worried that declining the invitation will lead to you no longer being invited to things in the future, then you can explicitly ask that they continue to invite you and even offer a vague time that they can try their request again. Try saying "I so appreciate you thinking of me, but I can't make it this time. But please do think of me in the future! Perhaps we can get together after the chaos of the holidays settles down."

THE BIGGEST HARD PLAN: CHRISTMAS DAY

Your hard plans will likely also include Christmas Eve or Christmas Day—especially if you are planning on seeing extended family this year. If you are planning to spend Christmas with just your immediate family, then your budget can be fairly low and it will be easier to keep your plan simple. But for many people, one or both of these days includes visiting and/or hosting extended family, and the money and time required for these special visits can be overwhelming if not planned for appropriately.

Purchasing and even making gifts takes time and money. Traveling to someone's home takes time and costs money (days off from work, gas, plane tickets, rental cars, etc). Cooking breakfast, brunch, lunch or dinner when hosting family also takes time and money. Sit down in advance of the big event and map out a realistic budget, craft your menu, set your parameters, create your boundaries, and delegate what you can.

Examples of this could be:
- We can visit my parents this year, and we'll visit your parents next year.
- We want to spend Christmas morning with our immediate family, but we can go to your parents for lunch.
- We can do Christmas Eve with my parents, and then Christmas Day with your parents.
- We can visit for Thanksgiving, but not for Christmas.
- Christmas morning will be just us and our kids. Extended family is welcome to join us later in the afternoon for lunch at our home.
- We will only purchase gifts for children 18 and under. We are not exchanging gifts for adults.
- We are only swapping books, and no other gifts.
- We are not exchanging any gifts, but we are all contributing to a family potluck dinner.
- We are drawing straws to decide which child each family is purchasing gifts for.

When it comes to budgeting, you'll need to go more in-depth with your plans:
- I'm hosting our family brunch and plan to make an omelette casserole and cinnamon rolls. I will delegate a fruit salad for one sister to bring, two gallons of OJ for my other sister to bring, my brother can bring two

bottles of inexpensive champagne, and my mother can bring her famous homemade hash browns. This gathering will cost us $35 in grocery supplies.

- It will cost $200 in gas for a round-trip car ride to visit our family that lives 7 hours away. We will also budget $20 in coffees, $40 in lunches. We will set our gift budget strictly at $100 and will draw a hard line in not spending any more than this and our total will be $360 for the weekend.

Figuring out your budget and time in advance will reduce a massive amount of stress. You will be able to spot items that are too expensive and too stressful and be able to gracefully decline them, even if it means not attending a large family gathering. Only you can determine what should have priority in this season; as everyone's personal situations are different. But really examine your plans and set your budgets for money and time sooner rather than later.

A COMMON HARD PLAN: VISITING SANTA:

For photos with Santa, I highly discourage going to the mall. While the malls usually have the most photo opportunities with plenty of available time slots, it is a consumerist trap! Once you are in the mall, you and/or your child will certainly find something to covet and eventually purchase. Instead, you can usually find Santa at the local tree-lighting ceremony at the town center, hospital lobbies, large hotel lobbies, farmer's markets, botanical gardens, local businesses, and more. Browse Facebook Events or post a question in a local online group and I can almost guarantee you there will be other opportunities to stand in a line (and often a much shorter one!) to let your child meet Santa and have their photo taken.

You can also hire a Santa yourself and have him visit your home for an annual Christmas Party treat! I have a friend who does this every year, often on Christmas Eve or the weekend before. The kindest, most realistic Santa surprises the children about thirty minutes into the party. He gives a booming "Ho, ho ho!" and takes a seat by my friend's family Christmas tree and one by one, the children warm up to him and eventually approach Santa on their own. Because it is in a private home and surrounded by friends they know, the experience truly feels magical. No one is waiting in a line with strangers. They are eating the cookies that everyone brought and ladling hot cocoa out of a crock pot. Children hide behind their parents' legs until they finally feel reassured that the man in red is safe for them to visit of their own volition.

An added benefit is that our host is also a professional photographer, so she snaps some fantastic candid photos of the children with Santa, and they seem so much more timeless and magical than a quick, posed—and often looking terrified—photo of a child, snapped by Mom on her smartphone. The adults discreetly drop a cash donation into a bucket that is passed around casually at the party and the donations all go to Santa. One year, we also gave donations to our photographer friend as well via her website afterward when she emailed the link for photos. This has been such a fantastic experience for my own family, that if this friend decided to no longer host her parties, I would gladly pick up the tradition and host one myself. If this sounds appealing to you, perhaps you would be interested in negotiating a Santa-for-hire or a Santa-for-donations Christmas party yourself!

LOOSE PLANS

"Loose plans" are exactly like they sound—plans that are very loosely scheduled. These are usually family traditions. You may be able to spot a possible weekend for holiday baking and cookie decorating. You might notice a possible weekend to drive an hour north to the nearest Christmas tree farm where you can chop your own tree. You might plan a weekend hiking in a snow-topped mountain or a weekend where you can drive around and look at Christmas lights in the surrounding neighborhoods. You might circle a date to have a Christmas movie marathon with cider and popcorn. Or there might be events in town that are intriguing options, but not something you want to fully commit to until the last minute (like a small "Maker's Festival" at the Farmers' Market, for example).

These are events that can happen on most any day, so if someone catches a cold or the vibe at home just doesn't match the plan, then keep yourself flexible and either scratch it altogether or move this loose plan to another day. Loose plans are adaptable and can be moved to another date if need be. While these plans for time with family are still a priority, simply knowing that they are not etched in stone can relieve a great deal of pressure.

I write "loose plans" in pencil on my paper calendar as well and in a different font or handwriting (such as italics or cursive) so that I can visually make these "loose plans" look different from the importance of the events with a hard date attached. I don't usually put these into my digital calendar. Personally, I prefer to have less alarms and notifications dinging from my phone's calendar. If I get an alert for a loose plan, it will feel more like a hard plan and may stress me out if it's not the right time to act on that plan. By glancing at a paper calendar with plans jotted in pencil, I am looking casually at my *options*, rather than being alerted to act. If I need to erase something or move the loose plan to another weekend, it feels easier to do it in pencil than trying to edit all of the criteria in a digital calendar.

After I am satisfied with the pacing of the "hard plans," it is easier to spot the open weekends that currently have no plans, or the longer stretches in the week that are not filled.

It may seem silly to pencil in loose plans, such as "bake sugar cookies," but during the holidays I have found this extremely helpful to keep from trying to do All The Things during the last week of Christmas. It's easier to "sprinkle in" the idyllic moments like making handmade Christmas cards, decorating gingerbread men, or watching your family's favorite holiday movie together. If you are not in control of the pacing, then there's a high chance you'll find yourself cramming in as much of these things as humanly possible into the last few days leading up to Christmas. Small children, husbands, teenagers—well, almost everyone—has a limited attention span for holiday activities, so spacing them out in an intentional way allows everyone to enjoy the sweet moment together, and then get back to the other things that are calling for their attention.

Now your calendar should be filled up with both loose and hard plans with a cushion of space in between. You know exactly how much or how little money you plan to spend on events. If you are struggling to think of loose plans, then let's move on to discussing family traditions in the next chapter.

5

CREATING TRADITIONS

What are your favorite memories of Christmas as a child? Take just a moment to close your eyes and pause from reading any further and quickly take a snapshot of your top three favorite memories with your family.

How many of those memories involved specific toys? ...I'm going to go out on a limb and bet that not many of those memories, if any at all, involved a detailed memory of a certain toy, much less every single toy or gift you ever received. Rather, most memories include the joy of doing something special with your family.

For me, one of my favorite memories is of our family driving around looking at Christmas lights—all three of us sisters staring out of the backseat window with a thermos of hot cocoa. Vince Guaraldi's jazz trio was bopping its classic Charlie Brown Christmas tunes in the background from the car radio. My sisters and I are all clamoring "Look to your left! The left, the LEFT!" "Oh my gosh, did you see the one on the RIGHT?! Right, right, right!" and a collective sigh of "Wowwww" as my father would slow the vehicle down to a crawl and let us bask in the twinkly glow of a particularly dressed up home in a subdivision where everyone was competing for the showiest light-show.

Another scene that flashes in my mind is decorating the tree. Everything about it was a tradition. Ceremoniously hauling the boxes from the attic, all three sisters plugging in each light strand to seriously examine the bulbs, and everyone claiming "their" ornaments and retelling the stories that went with each one. You see, we had a tradition of each getting an ornament every year that represented something that happened that year (for example, the year I studied abroad and traveled to Paris, my mother gave me a hand-blown Eiffel Tower ornament). With The Temptations Christmas album blaring on the stereo, my father lay on the couch and watched the scene with a smile on his face and instructed us where "his" ornaments should go. His duties were to saw off the end of the tree and straighten it in the stand, while my mom stood back directing miniscule adjustments to the left and right until it was absolutely perfect. Once the tree was fully decorated, my father dramatically put the angel on top as the grand finale, after each of us gave her a little kiss.

You might say "*Hey! You had a lot of boxes! You purchased annual ornaments! That's a lot of things! That's not minimalist!*" Yes, my mother was and still is a maximalist. However, I want to remind you that what really matters is pursuing an *intentional* Christmas. If you cut out all the extraneous things pulling you in a hundred directions, then you can focus on the magical moments you spend together.

And yes, that can include a fully decked-out Christmas tree, as long as it is your *intent* and something the whole family embraces as a part of their story. (Conversely, if you or your family feel pressured to go all out on the Christmas tree, out of habit or to live up to cultural norms, and the "tradition" feels stressful, then I think it would be wise to step back and take a simpler approach.)

And, while that was a fond memory from my childhood and a wonderful tradition, I've decided not to replicate it with my own family. At least, not in this season. My family is organically shaping its own story, and right now, it requires very few ornaments. I do try to capture that flavor of my own childhood memories by including the children in every aspect of putting up our simple tree.

I'm giving this personal example to help guide you in identifying the traditions that you loved as a child and to give you the permission you might need to either embrace it for your own or nix it.

If you are searching for a simpler, more memorable holiday to bring your family closer this year, then creating strong traditions will be a central part. Below I will list out a variety of traditions that you might consider, or perhaps they are things you already do and did not think of as a tradition. When looking at this list, if you feel like you already do every single one of these items, you might consider scaling back and dropping a few, especially if the holiday season seems overwhelming. This list is NOT a checklist of things you should do. Rather, I'd consider focusing on only three or four things. This list is simply a brainstorming session laid out for those who really need some ideas for things to incorporate that don't include consumerist traditions like gift shopping at the mall.

SUGGESTIONS FOR SIMPLE TRADITIONS

Picking out the Christmas Tree. Whether you are selecting a live one from the lot or headed out into the woods to chop one down yourself, this can be such a fun activity for everyone in the family to join in on together. Explain to children the height and width you are all searching for, and hang back and smile as they examine every tree on the lot to see if it fits the specifications. *"Too tall; too skinny; too bare; too full..."* It's fun for children and adults alike to run around in a forest or a lot of trees and make judgement calls. Show the kids how to run their hands gently along a branch. If their hand is full of needles, the tree will die soon; and if their hand is quite empty, then it's a healthy one. They will enjoy becoming wise connoisseurs of Christmas trees. If you select one that they have deemed perfect, they will beam with pride! The entire process can be exciting—from watching the stump get trimmed with a chainsaw to strapping the tree onto the roof of the car. Even if you prefer to have a faux tree at home, it can still be fun to wander the Christmas Tree lots with children and let them breathe in that fantastic evergreen scented air! You can pick up tree trimmings (sometimes they give those away for free!) and set them around your house to bring that delightful scent into every room. Some tree lots give away hot cocoa or cider, or you can plan to bring your own. My family had a tradition of doing this on the first day after Thanksgiving. Because there was a special date attached to it, it became the most anticipated tradition of all.

Decorating the Tree and Home. Let this be a family event! Let go of the perfectionist in yourself and let the kids have fun. (You can always redo and fix things discreetly at a later time, if necessary). Everyone will have a different approach and style, but if your family is included in every step along the way, each moment will likely start to feel like a tradition.

Hot Drinks. As mentioned above, adding hot drinks to any event instantly makes it feel more festive, warms your hands, and heats you up from the inside out. I like to set up a hot cocoa bar in my kitchen—similar to a coffee bar or cocktail bar. I have special holiday mugs and containers for ingredients or packets, and a large jar of mini-marshmallows and candy canes. It's not extremely extravagant, but having it gathered together in plain view helps me to easily add a holiday drink to our activities. My mother started a tradition of making *wassail* when guests were over—usually for Christmas Day. It's a traditional English drink that is similar to apple cider, but with more spices mulled. It can be brewed on the stove or in a crock pot. A bottle of port sat next to the pot for adults who wanted to add a splash of merriment to their cup. Another friend has a tradition of offering all adults at her party a cup of *Gluehwein*. This is a German/Austrian winter drink that most tourists know as an "after-ski" drink. It is a brew of spices such as cloves and cardamom, sugar, cinnamon, zest of lemon and orange, then mulled in red wine and brandy in a pot over a hot stove. Winter drinks smell like the holidays, taste divine, and can quickly warm you up. Try incorporating them into your family traditions. Perhaps you set up a mulled apple station for a non-alcohol option for children and guests, and a gluehwein pot for those who wish to imbibe. For any holiday outing with children, you can add hot cocoa or hot apple cider to a thermos to add a little more specialness to the event. (*You can find recipes in my free ebook! Link at the end of book*).

Looking at lights. Grab that thermos, turn on a great Christmas album and simply drive around to the neighborhoods and subdivisions who love to decorate! This is a very simple, easy and potentially free event to make into a tradition if you bundle up and take bikes or go for a stroll (or the price of gas if you take a car). They can even be wearing their cozy Christmas pajamas, so if the slow ride puts the children to sleep, you can simply lay them in bed afterward. There are often churches, botanical gardens, and town squares that are decorated to the hilt. You can search online for special drives where an entire mile or more of lights will be synchronized to holiday music—often found in larger cities, and with an entrance fee.

Go for a winter hike. Another inexpensive or free tradition is to have an annual winter hike. Perhaps you wait for the first snow. Perhaps it's a certain trail you visit for this annual tradition. Perhaps it is done on Christmas Eve or Christmas Day. You get to set the parameters (or even better, let those parameters reveal themselves organically over time).

Attend a town holiday event. Be careful not to try and make every town event a tradition. This could easily become overwhelming and is something I was guilty of attempting early on in motherhood. Town events are often something such as: an annual Christmas Tree lighting in the town square; a holiday arts & crafts festival; Santa visits/photographs; a Christmas Parade; a decorated sailboat parade; a holiday marathon; a holiday circus; holiday historic home tours; and other similar public events. Just pick one or two that get your family the most excited and make it a goal to attend every year. Be flexible and don't guilt yourself if you miss a year here and there.

Celebrate your Religion or Spirituality. You may have traditions that help you focus on the spiritual meaning of Christmas in the Christian faith, such as: family prayer time, midnight mass, church services, Advent, creating a nativity scene, or visiting a live nativity scene. You may choose to celebrate other religious or cultural holiday traditions during the month of December or January such as Hanukkah (Jewish), Pancha Ganapati (Hindu), Solstice (Pagan), Kwanzaa (African-American Culture), and others. Families who don't belong to a church or other religious background may want to establish their own rituals that embody the spirit of kindness and togetherness.

Go ice skating. Whether you have an idyllic frozen pond in your town or you visit the local hockey rink, this could be such a fun and energetic activity for you and the kids!

Play in the snow. If you're lucky enough to live in a place with white winters, get outdoors and take a moment to really appreciate it. Pack some snowballs up and have a snowball fight. Invite the neighbors. Lay down and make snow angels. Roll up some big balls and make a snowman together. Engage with your children and take advantage of this free fun stuff that only lasts a few hours or a few months.

Attend a holiday arts event. Most cities have an arts community that performs classics annually, such as The Nutcracker Ballet. Professional and community orchestras and jazz bands usually perform a Christmas concert. Adult and children's theatres often put on a production such as The Night Before Christmas or The Grinch Who Stole Christmas. Even art galleries and "art crawls" often incorporate a holiday theme. Look at your local arts calendar and you'll be delighted at all of the fantastic events offered for a small ticket price or sometimes even for free. Don't underestimate your child's interest and ability to attend an arts event. Depending on their age, even the smallest child can hold an attention span for the first half of a show. Pro tip: If you have very young children, keep expectations low, be flexible and prepared to only see one half of the show together. Purchase seats at the end of a row, so that you can easily sneak out if little ones get too unruly. Remember, this is about being joyful, present and together. Leave *before* it gets stressful, embarrassing, or frustrating. You'll know when that moment arrives. Even just half of a show can be an amazing experience and develop an appreciation for the arts.

Bake together, and pick a favorite recipe. Baking is such a fun and easy experience, as you don't have to leave the house! Spend a few years trying out different recipes until you discover the family hits and eventually your kids will request to make a particular type of goodie each year. The basics to try are chocolate chip cookies, sugar cookies, gingerbread cookies, and gingerbread houses. Baking is a wonderful opportunity to allow children (and adults!) a chance to exercise their creativity with cookie cutters and icing, candy, and sprinkles to decorate. You could try to make pies with pretty designs on the crust. Or hop onto Pinterest or Google to discover hundreds of fantastic, more elaborate recipes centered around a holiday theme. If you have ample sweets filling up your home, consider teaching your kids about the spirit of giving and bundle some up to give to neighbors, teachers, friends and family. Your children will be delighted to give something they helped create themselves. A tradition of giving is an excellent tradition that teaches generosity and character.

My family's baking traditions

My favorite baking tradition from my own childhood was a cookie called "Santa's Forgotten Cookies." It was a fascinating concept as a child because you whipped up the "dough" (meringue), baked it a low temp for a few hours, and then turned the oven off and left the cookies in the oven overnight to "finish baking." We did this on Christmas Eve and then were delighted to open up the oven and discover they were fully baked on Christmas Day. Hence the name, Santa's "Forgotten" Cookies. It seemed like magic! (*Download my free e-book for this recipe! Link at the end of this book.*)

Another simple baking tradition my mother started and that I have continued is to have cinnamon rolls with orange icing on Christmas Day while opening up gifts. Having cinnamon rolls for breakfast has always been a rare treat and rolls with orange icing is even rarer—in fact,

I've only ever had it on Christmas, so the association is now strong. As a mother myself, I realized that the creation of this tradition is brilliant. It takes one minute to take pre-made cinnamon rolls out of the carton and to stick them in an oven to bake for a few minutes. There is no prep work required or actual baking skills. Sure, you could make cinnamon rolls from scratch, but the idea behind this is to be *present* for the gift-opening excitement and not busy working in the kitchen and missing all the fun expressions and happy hugs. A delightful treat of sugary breakfast is made in a matter of minutes and all you have to do is take them out of the oven and transfer them onto plates. Now you can sit back on the floor with your little ones and help them tear open boxes.

Perhaps you can create a similar tradition. Even pre-making a healthy quiche the night before that you can simply stick in the oven could create the same sort of ease as my mother's cinnamon roll tradition.

Watching Christmas movies and reading Christmas books together. Over the years, you'll discover which holiday movies are family favorites and can create scheduled or impromptu movie marathon nights. Add hot cocoa, cookies or popcorn and it's instantly special! Add a basket or shelf in the living room with a collection of Christmas books, or make a special trip to the library. Cuddle on the couch with a cozy throw blanket by the twinkly light of the Christmas tree and you've created a special moment together.

Volunteer for a Charity. There are ample opportunities to model the giving spirit of the holidays to your children. It could be as simple as plunking a dollar into a bell-ringing Salvation Army Santa's bucket. You could have the children help unload the boxes and bags of toys you decluttered and bring them to the donation drop-off site as a family. You could gather canned goods from the pantry together to donate to a shelter. You could shop for a child in need by contributing to an "Angel Tree" or similar type charity. You could volunteer to serve lunch at a soup kitchen together or pack supplies at a food pantry. You could declutter your extra blankets and coats and bring them to a homeless shelter. The list is endless. Take some time to figure out what needs you could help fulfill in your community and make it a family event.

Again, this is not a checklist of things you have to do, but rather a list of examples intended to be inspiring. And there are so many more traditions one could create beyond just these. It is my hope that these general ideas get your creative juices flowing as you pay attention to the types of things your family enjoys doing together. Just remember that the focus is to be present and joyful. If anything starts to feel forced, overwhelming, chaotic or overly stressful, then take a step back, figure out what elements are contributing to that feeling...and then adjust. Remain open to removing that event altogether for the sake of sanity and peace.

As mentioned in Chapter 4, if your events ("hard plans" and "loose plans") are mapped out in advance and given space for a comfortable, slow pace, then hopefully you'll find that traditions such as the ones mentioned above are given the room they need to grow organically.

DROPPING SELF-IMPOSED TRADITIONS

As a brand-new mother, I was determined to build purposeful traditions for my newly growing family, but went a bit overboard for the first few years. I wanted so badly for our town's sailboat parade to be a family tradition, since it was unique to the town we lived in. However, my husband's company always scheduled the company holiday party for the same evening. For the first two years I forced my poor husband to stand in the freezing cold wind to watch the decorated sailboats float by with an irritable baby strapped to my chest. We couldn't enjoy the parade because we were so anxious about when we should leave and head to the party. We were late to the holiday party because of the event and therefore anxious on the drive there and fumbling to find our dinner seats once we arrived, feeling a bit disoriented for the entire party. I finally caved on the third and fourth year and decided to drop the sailboat parade "tradition" in order to make the holiday party event a less stressful event. While we achieved an easier experience, we eventually realized it was not as necessary for his career to attend it as we originally thought it was and decided the sailboat parade—and nothing else—will be how we spend that weekend in the future. We pivoted, and we will pivot again.

I wanted to share this experience to remind you to stay flexible while trying to establish traditions. Don't create a more stressful experience for your entire family simply for tradition's sake. If there is a conflict, it's okay. You can miss a tradition for a few years and pick it back up later if/when it makes more sense.

Also, consider each thing objectively and decide whether "mandatory" events truly are required, or if it is a self-imposed expectation, as in the case of a company party.

Another version of a self-imposed tradition is often the holiday greeting card. For some people, this might be a wonderful experience. But if you bemoan the time and cost involved in scheduling a professional photo shoot, wrangling and bribing kids into a forced smile, buying or coordinating outfits, choosing your graphic design, writing out individual addresses and stocking up on stamps, then remembering to actually mail them… then you should give yourself some grace and skip this cultural phenomenon. It can be very costly and time-consuming and, more often than not, is a massive source of stress.

Evaluate whether you are forcing this tradition on yourself and your family and why. Perhaps you drop this tradition altogether. Perhaps you should opt for a simpler tradition, such as hand-made cards from the kids that were the result of a peaceful day of crafting together. Perhaps you only make a dozen for immediate family, instead of mailing every person you've ever befriended. Perhaps you order a custom stamp or stickers with your home address on it. Perhaps you create a spreadsheet of addresses and simply print the addresses onto envelopes. Find ways to automate the stressful elements, and figure out the balance that fits your family in this season of life. Take the load off of yourself if it is feeling too heavy.

6

BUYING (LESS) GIFTS

An integral part of creating a more intentional, minimal holiday is getting the gift-giving aspect of Christmas under control. As you read in Chapter 2, western culture is spending a LOT of money for Christmas. It's a global issue, but the U.S. is particularly guilty of overindulgence. In the film of the popular children's book "Harry Potter and the Sorcerer's Stone" by J.K. Rowling, there's an opening scene where a young boy named Dudley is celebrating his 12th birthday and surveying a room full of gifts. The conversation is one that will ring familiar to most parents' nightmarish fears of letting a child down on Christmas morning:

Dudley : *How many are there?*

Father : *36, counted them myself.*

Dudley : *36! But last year, last year I had 37!*

Father : *Yes, yes, but some of them are quite a bit bigger than last year.*

Dudley : *I don't care how big they are!*

Many of us are guilty of spoiling our children, as we live in a world of abundance. We want to give our children the world. We want to make sure each Christmas is more magical than the last. We want them to feel satisfied and ecstatic, not disappointed. Armies of marketing geniuses have tried to brainwash us into believing that our children need more, newer, better, bigger, flashier items.

Technology has trapped us with its caches of search history, data collection, personalization, and algorithms that recommend to us the next "perfect gift" every time we look at our device. Even if we resist an impulse purchase at that very moment, we might find that we "star," "favorite," "pin," and "add to cart" in order to consider (and likely purchase) these recommended trendy gifts at a later date. Add a tempting sale, like the ones promoted on "Black Friday" and "Cyber Monday," and we might discover 37 boxes on our doorstep the following morning.

After we've stashed the 37 boxes in the depths of our closet, we realize that we forgot the stockings. And so 50 more "small" purchases here and there for cheap odds and ends quickly compound into a hefty and unplanned lump sum in itself.

Does any of this sound familiar to you? This was certainly my reality as a new mother, anyways.

So how do we cut back? How do we become more intentional with our gift-giving and our spending?

STRATEGY #1, BUDGET

One obvious way would be to set a strict budget. But budgets can vary from household to household and you might be tempted to purchase many cheaper items rather than a few quality items. This strategy can be more helpful to you if you layer it with some of the other strategies listed below.

STRATEGY #2, THE 4-GIFT RULE

A popular way for minimalists to approach a drastic decrease in gift-giving is to put some guidelines in place that dictate what can be purchased and what amount. Over the past decade, a certain rhyme has become increasingly accepted as a great baseline:

Something you want,

Something you need,

Something to wear,

Something to read.

This places parameters around the type of items that are gifted and sets up expectations for kids and loved ones. It is up to you who these gifts are from—the parents or "Santa." Also, this guideline is intended to be used for your immediate household (not to be imposed on your extended family). Four gifts are actually quite enough. We've become so accustomed to excess, that hitting the brakes and declaring "The 4-Gift Rule" might feel jarring for many people.

As a society we've adjusted to a hedonic lifestyle—one where we seek increasingly more pleasure out of life, justifying the purchase of expensive items, seeking attention (think of social media), a tendency to act impulsively, a tendency to not think rationally, a tendency to follow and be easily influenced, an urge to collect luxury and tech items, and a tendency to want an item spontaneously. As hedonists, we have a view of life that considers pleasure to be the main purpose of life. In regards to the holidays, this mindset has gotten completely out of control.

The 4-Gift Rule helps recalibrate to just a few items that can truly spark joy and are not simply "wants" but also "needs." While it may be hard to fathom, you and your children will adjust more easily than you think. Hedonic adaptation is the proven tendency of humans' ability to quickly return to a relatively stable level of happiness despite life's ups and downs. For example, someone could lose their entire home and all of their belongings in a tornado or fire, and yet a year later discover that they are incredibly happy and adjusted to their new way of life.

In this case, you are intentionally creating a "down" by purposely capping the amount of items entering your home. Because there are so few items allowed within the boundaries of this poem, you are likely to put much more consideration into the quality of the items. With higher quality items that fulfill a specific purpose in your lives, you will likely experience much more joy each time you use, wear or read one of these items. You adapt to less and experience an increase in joy (and a decrease in stress, and an increase in your bank account…resulting in even more delight!).

I've focused more on this strategy rather than simply trying to stick to a budget, because I believe these parameters help curate a better overall experience and help align values with a dose of "essentialism" (eliminating non-essentials) by only allowing one true "want."

I frequently get asked several questions regarding this strategy:

How do I make the switch to The 4-Gift Rule after previously setting expectations of "large" Christmases?

This nail-biting question is usually in reference to parents of children. It may be that your children—like Dudley in our opening example—are used to their Christmases getting bigger and better with each year. Their expectation is to find a Christmas tree with so many gifts spilling out from beneath it, that they may be overtaking the whole room. How do you prepare them for four simple packages?

First, if you are able to make more time for rituals and traditions as discussed in the previous chapter, then the focus on presents can shift instead to these cherished moments. Emphasizing the magical time of year can help take pressure off of the gifts aspect.

If your child is very little (toddler to elementary school-aged), I recommend that the change "come from Santa." I've written an accompanying children's book on this premise, where Santa and his elves are overwhelmed by the sheer volume of requests coming in from children's letters. Simultaneously, the "Joy-O-Meter" is showing that the children are not feeling very happy. Santa, Mrs. Claus, and the head elves determine that new guidelines will need to be set for all future Letters to Santa, or else they'll simply have to cancel Christmas. Santa mails a letter to all of the children of the world to gently inform them of "The 4-Gift Rule" and asks that they put careful consideration into their requests as they fill out their "one want, one need, something to wear, and something to read." You'll find a link to my children's book at the end—or simply borrow this idea and create your own story around Santa and his gift-giving process.

If your child is in middle school or high school, then sitting them down for a more rational, adult conversation is probably a better route. Are they environmentally conscious children? Then perhaps focus more on the environmental impact of production and shipping costs as well as the waste in our landfills. Talking through the mental benefits of reducing anxiety by decluttering and paring our items down to what we truly want and need may make sense to more mature children who are acutely feeling the stress and pressures of young adulthood. If you have a parenting rule of "clean up your room before you do anything else," then demonstrate to them how much more quickly their room will be cleaned when it is not filled to the brim with items that need to be managed. Less things equals more freedom!

I wouldn't, however, approach it from a scarcity mindset—such as "we don't have the money for more than four things." If you want to be inclusive about finances with your children (which is wise, if done appropriately), then you could discuss it in a way that teaches how savings can turn into growing investments. It can be a great segue into teaching financial literacy, and showing how discipline can eventually grow into financial freedom. You can give examples of how indulging every desire can deplete all savings and send a person into debt. The compounding interest can make them a slave to the "hamster wheel" many adults find themselves in: working for money to pay for things and all their related costs.

Who makes the list?

Again, this part of The 4-Gift Rule is open to interpretation and varies with age and circumstances. If your child is very little, then you fulfill the four items for your child. If your child is a toddler or elementary school-aged, then you may present it to them as "What is the one thing you really want?" and then you (or "Santa") fulfill the other three items. For older children, I would let them decide if they would like to have input on one or all of the four items. Some of them might say "surprise me!" You might just eavesdrop on your child as they sit in Santa's lap to take a photo. You might ask them a few times over the course of the holidays to hone in on their desires. You might present them with stationery and an envelope to mail to the North Pole—and make a tradition of it! How you go about implementing The 4-Gift Rule is up to you.

STRATEGY #3, QUALITY OVER QUANTITY

This strategy easily fits in with #1 (Budget) and #2 (The 4-Gift Rule), but as it is an expression on intentionality, it must be discussed by itself. Minimalism can mean not only paring items down, but also making sure that the items we keep in the house are of a high quality that will bring joy over a long time. Minimalism can be a frugal way of life if you're not constantly exchanging worn out items with cheap replacements.

Focus on classic items that are not susceptible to trends. A super simple, higher-end black dress that you know complements your body shape will last for decades in your closet, as opposed to a cheaply made, inexpensive dress with floral prints and trendy frills. Develop a discerning eye for simplicity and classic designs for everything from children's toys to furniture and tech gadgets. Can you envision the four gifts you are planning to give to someone all lasting in joy, usefulness, and durability for the next five years? If so, you've found quality pieces.

Another way to detect quality is to consider an item's sustainability. This may be of more importance to some than others; but being eco-friendly is one of my values. Choose natural materials over plastic. Consider the entire lifespan of an object—including how many hundreds or thousands of years it may take for an item to break down in a landfill or in what other ways this item will compound negatively for the planet and thus, human life. If an item is made out of plastic, try searching for an alternative made from material such as glass, metal or wood. Even cling-wrap for your Christmas cookies could be replaced with cloth and beeswax, and single-use storage bags can be replaced with long-lasting silicone bags.

Take it a step further and consider the ethicalness of the item's production. Was it hand-made by someone who is improving their life with honest work? Or were they paid pennies in a chemical-laden sweatshop? Did they test the items on animals or source the materials from animals?

Being careful not to collect clutter, you could consider buying items second hand. Thrift shops, yard sales, eBay, and Facebook Marketplace may have just the item you were searching for in good condition, and it delays the item going into the landfill for just a bit longer. Recycling, repurposing and reusing are great ways to be both frugal and sustainable with gift-giving.

Consider the ingredients of things you buy this holiday—such as food, soaps or candles. Are there harmful dyes or perfumes? Do you understand the ingredients listed on the back? What are you ingesting, inhaling, or rubbing on your body? Or, what are you giving as a gift to someone to put in or on their body? Align your personal values with your pocketbook.

For children, it has been proven that more open-ended toys foster play, creativity and imagination. Exercising this "creative muscle" is crucial for their development and eventual success as an adult. Besides cardboard boxes, sticks and rocks, some of the best open-ended toys that allow room for exploring their imagination are building blocks, play kitchens, animal figurines, doll play, miniature automobile play, dress up/role play, and sensory items. The Montessori approach is to use safe, natural materials (namely wood), very little color or stimulation, no blinky lights or noises/music, no cartoon characters or corporate imagery. This approach emphasizes wooden toys with simple moving parts like wheels, rope and elegant shapes kept in an uncluttered environment to reduce overwhelm. I recommend considering these qualifications for quality when purchasing a child's gift this Christmas.

What about invitations to gift exchanges?

My advice is to "Just Say No." Use the examples discussed in Chapter 4 to politely decline from "Dirty Santa", "Secret Santa" and "White Elephant" type holiday gift exchanges. You are the only person in control of what items come into your household (and what types of items you spend your hard-earned money on). Usually these types of exchanges come with $10 or $20 price limits and the items are usually generic, cheap, or plain silly. It's an easy way to have yet another item enter your home that you would not intentionally use. Before you know it, you will have accumulated all sorts of things that need decluttering.

Granted, while I suggest declining an event that encourages purchasing and bringing home possible clutter, you might find that events like these are still worth participating in if purchasing only one gift releases you from any obligation to purchase more gifts for each individual. Or perhaps it truly is a group of people that would bring you joy to spend time with. In cases like these, then purchase the most useful gift you can contribute to the party and choose wisely.

You could also suggest a "present truce" with close friends to help ease the stress that comes with gift-giving obligations. Perhaps you bake items for one another or give a small handmade token, but there is no expectation of reciprocation.

If you want to avoid gift exchanges, but would like to take the initiative to hold a fun gathering with your friends, perhaps try a "Cookie Swap" instead. This encourages each person to bake something handmade and creative—a rewarding experience in itself. Each household goes home with a variety of interesting baked goods to sample in the weeks leading to Christmas. Another variation of this is a "Handmade Ornament Swap."

An event I enjoy hosting is a "Vision Board Party" with my best friends just after the Christmas holidays. Everyone brings a poster board, glue, scissors, and a stack of magazines. They could also contribute a snack or a bottle of wine and this "potluck craft party" turns into an enlightening experience as everyone snips away at imagery and words that capture the visions each guest has for their New Year. These collages can reveal a lot to each person to help them find what aspirations they may have, and be surprisingly clearer than a New Year Resolution.

Get creative about finding ways to nudge your own circle into experiences and traditions that don't include mindlessly purchasing material items that will clutter your homes.

7

FOCUSING ON PRESENCE, NOT PRESENTS

The modern world is full of deadlines and obligations. It holds speed and efficiency in high esteem. This busyness seems to grow exponentially as we enter the holiday season. We feel that we can accomplish more by tackling tasks two or three at a time. But this multi-tasking comes at a high price.

Another mindset shift that will be needed in order to achieve an intentional, minimal Christmas is to fight the urge to multi-task and fall in line with the frenetic pace of the world around you.

Time is our most precious commodity. Too many of us are chasing money and objects, and are missing out on the true wealth in life. Our days are packed, schedules are over-loaded, and we tell ourselves we have "no free time." Even when we achieve a decent savings in our bank account, we don't have the free time to enjoy it! Victims of mindlessness, distraction, and ambition, we get lost in a cycle of pursuing "more, more, more." This leads to us living lives that are more impoverished than those who have far less than us. In our pursuit of achievement, we've lost our balance with happiness and calm contentment.

Pause. Take a slow, deep breath.

Are you here, in the now? Or are you divided and mentally somewhere else? People around you are talking, but are you listening? Are you thinking about what will happen tomorrow? Or what will happen 10 minutes from now?

If you keep experiencing that division, you will miss a lot. Our days are limited and our hours are precious. Decide right now who and what you care about, and how you want to allocate your time to make those people and things your priority.

In order to do that, you have to slow down. Slow way down.

Put away your digital devices. Listen to what your loved ones are saying. Slow your breathing. Slow your reactions. Slow your walking. Slow your eating. Savor everything you've got before it's all gone.

Living slowly and intentionally will help you to live contentedly. Among the things we value the most are love, friendship, beauty, solace and humor. When we are living our life at a slower pace we can enjoy these things all the more. When we slow down, we enhance our gratitude and experience greater physical and mental health. We can appreciate the beauty around us and connect with people on a deeper level. Slowing down allows us to get control of our life.

GET GROUNDED

When I find I need to quiet my mind and become more present, I try this simple meditation or grounding exercise, called the "5,4,3,2,1 technique." I've found it a helpful tool when needing to relax and come back to the present. It essentially allows you to become hyper-aware by using your senses:

1. **Five** things you can see, described in detail
2. **Four** things you can feel
3. **Three** things you can hear
4. **Two** things you can smell
5. **One** thing you can taste (or 1 good thing about yourself)

To give a quick example of each of these items:

1. "I can see red hibiscus flowers outside of the window screen, with a bumblebee nestled in the pollen" x5
2. "I can feel the air coming in and out of my nose" x4
3. "I can hear a lawnmower in the distance" x3
4. "I can smell my coffee" x2
5. "I can taste the honey in my coffee" or "I love my ability to make my kids laugh"

You should feel calmer and more at ease by the end of this exercise and incredibly present. I find that the effects of this last for quite a while afterward, and I become more aware of the world around me by using all of my senses intentionally, and therefore start brimming with gratitude. I hope that this exercise helps ground you in the present as well.

When the flurry of events, deadlines, and obligations start whirling around you during the holidays, take just a moment to ground yourself. You will then feel the weight lift off of you as you are better able to see what is in your control, and what is worth your time and attention.

DIGITAL DECLUTTER

"Digital Minimalism" is a new term being introduced in the minimalist space, and championed by author Cal Newport with his book under the same name. If you feel that much of your distraction, stress or overwhelm is stemming from the digital world—email, inboxes, notifications, apps, social media, smartphones, tablets, computers—then I recommend taking a deep dive into ways that you can unplug. He outlines mindset shifts and practical tips for cutting out the noise of this added dimension to our modern world. If your current relationship with technology is unsustainable, then the holidays are a great time to cut down on the aspects that no longer "spark joy," as famous minimalist Marie Kondo has coined.

As the holidays ramp up, images from Instagram influencers cleverly display new must-have items in their perfectly edited and curated photographs. Pinterest recommends visual imagery of perfectly decorated living rooms with coordinated decorations and well-behaved children snuggled by the fireplace. Facebook newsfeeds seem to shout at you to do more as every person you've ever met chronicles every holiday experience they have. Year-end deadlines make email inboxes explode with urgency. Promotional emails add to the inbox even more. Amazon recommends a multitude of "perfect gifts" at tempting price points. Sales notifications buzz your phone until it sounds like a kazoo. A simple glance at our smartphone can be all it takes to feel "not-enoughness" or "FOMO/fear of missing out." You are enough and you have enough. Don't let the tools inside your phone convince you otherwise.

Now would be a good time to consider deleting or disabling apps, turning off notifications, setting limits on social media use, and unsubscribing from promotional emails. We live in such a noisy, distracting world as it is—don't let digital distraction steal from your presence and joy, too.

A CHILDLIKE VIEW

If you have younger children, consider yourself very lucky, as you have access to an incredible mentor for becoming more present. Children are naturally aware of the finer details in life.

My toddlers gasp when they see a bird take flight and pause to stare, point, and exclaim in wonder at the phenomenon. My youngest child currently giggles in triumphant delight every time she is able to fill her spoon up successfully with rice. They splash their bathwater with enthusiasm, reveling in the magic of physics. They dance with abandon. An expanse of grass calls for running barefoot, and wildflower weeds are gathered into scraggly bouquets and placed into crystal vases, as if they were the finest of flowers. Tap into that childlike view of the world and try seeing your surroundings as if you were a child. Dig deep to rediscover your sense of awe, appreciation and joy in the simplest of things.

8

ASKING YOUR FAMILY (TO NOT BUY STUFF)

You may feel comfortable with the number of items you personally allow to come through your door throughout the year, but when the holidays come around, you are suddenly no longer the only purchaser of items that enter your family's space. What about all the gifts that aren't coming from your own bank account?

Many of the belongings in your home that you recently decluttered were likely the result of gifts. You may even be able to identify one or a few main culprits for the onslaught of material items—usually a grandmother, aunt, uncle or best friend. Before you begrudge these Gift Givers' past generosity, let's focus on how to positively approach the matter for the future, as well as embrace a mindset change that keeps your emotions joyful throughout the holiday.

Family dynamics can be hard to navigate, and every family is so different and comes with its own history and varied personalities. There isn't any one-size-fits-all advice; however, I think it's safe to say that a hard message of, "*Do not buy us stuff*" will not go down well. The Gift Giver obviously cares for you and your family, and has sought giving gifts as a means to show that to you. If you say, "*We're minimalists now. Stop buying things for us. I'm just going to get rid of it if you do*," you are unlikely to keep a pleasant and healthy relationship.

In Gary Chapman's book "The Five Love Languages," he identifies the five ways that most people give and receive the message of love: words of affirmation, acts of service, quality time, physical touch, and *receiving/giving gifts*. It's important to recognize that the people who are guilty of bringing in truckloads of gifts each Christmas are expressing their love in the best way they know how. It is the "language" that they best understand and speak. When you add a big dose of cultural expectations, brilliant holiday marketing and consumerist messaging, the Gift Giver is likely to go overboard and shower you in their "love language."

When you approach the Gift Giver(s) in your life, be kind and be flexible. I have three strategies for how to address minimalism this Christmas with a Gift Giver.

STRATEGY #1, DROPPING HINTS

You may take an approach where you casually share your view of things in your home and share the positive effects that decluttering has had in your life. Be careful not to point any fingers at the source of these things (the Gift Giver) or to word it in a way that shames or guilts them. An example script would be:

Gift Giver: *How are you doing?*

You: Great! *I was feeling overwhelmed but now I've done a massive declutter and donated all the stuff we didn't need. It's made such a big difference. I'm able to spend more time with the kids and I think everyone is happier.*

Gift Giver: *That sounds great! I'm so glad to hear you're feeling better and that the kids are doing well. It's wonderful you can spend more time with them.*

You: *Yes! We've all benefited from decluttering. I'm feeling a little nervous about Christmas, though, and undoing all the hard work once, ahem, Santa arrives… haha!*

Gift Giver: *Oh yes! There will always be more!*

You: *Yeah… I'm hoping to cut way back this year. We're not planning on spending very much, and we've told the kids about the "4-Gift Rule" and they are totally on board. Have you heard of it?*

Gift Giver: *No, what is that?*

You: *It's a cute little rhyme, but it sets a healthy guideline so that we don't go overboard. It goes, "Something you want, something you need, something you wear, something you read."*

Gift Giver: *Ah… that's cute.*

You: *Yeah, it really just helps us reign it in. Experience gifts are a good way to do that, too, I hear. You know, like museum tickets, zoo passes, bowling alley gift cards. That sort of stuff.*

Gift Giver: *Oh, that's a good idea!*

You see? That wasn't a painful conversation. There was no serious intervention needed. You don't have to use fancy words like "minimalism" and spout off any definitions. You're simply sharing your efforts and your pain points, then sharing how much smoother your household is running after decluttering. Then you plant the seeds of how they could still give gifts, but in a more intentional way or in a way that doesn't take up square footage in your home. You never identified them as a particular source of incoming material items or related stress. You kept the conversation inclusive and light-hearted.

Obviously I can't map out precisely how a conversation will play out, but this gives you a possible idea of language and approach.

STRATEGY #2, SET LIMITS

Another approach is to set guidelines or limits for the entire extended family. Create a guideline that everyone feels comfortable with such as "We are only gifting books this year," "Only one toy per grandchild," or "We're drawing straws to determine which family buys gifts for another family," or "Nothing over $50." Bring up the conversation with your family and you might be surprised how relieved everyone is to have permission to simplify as well.

STRATEGY #3, PROVIDE LISTS

If you know the Gift Giver will not be on board with gifting experiences, then try creating an Amazon Wishlist or Pinterest Board or some other digital list where you collect and link the material items that you would appreciate receiving. Perhaps you just decluttered a lot of blinking, music-making, bright-colored plastic toys, and would like to be very intentional about only introducing wooden, eco-friendly, open-ended toys that allow your child to use their imagination and creativity. Include the Gift Giver in a conversation about this intentional change and offer suggestions/recommendations by sending them the link to this wishlist. If items are certain to still enter your home, then at least give them the opportunity to purchase gifts that you will all love.

EXPECT GIFTS

The next step is to lower your expectations. It's not likely you will be able to change a Gift Giver—especially not after only one conversation or after one holiday. It may take a few years for this person to observe your household with its new lifestyle to understand what it means and what types of gifts you would appreciate the most. It may also take a few years of them observing how often you declutter the house and playroom to recognize that material gifts won't survive for long in your household. Eventually, they may understand that they can still receive the amazing rush of dopamine and oxytocin (the chemicals that trigger the feelings of love and happiness) by expressing their "love language" of Gift Giving... but by giving the gift of *experiences* instead of material items.

Then again, they may never come to that understanding and may never change their ways. And I know that this can be a major source of frustration and tension, especially in minimalist households. In fact, some Gift Givers tend to give even *more*, when they misunderstand the benefits of minimalism (*"Those kids don't have enough!" "I don't want their Christmas to be disappointing by only getting four things!" "Your house is so cold and bare!"*) Don't demonize them and convince yourself that they are bringing gifts purely to undermine your decluttering efforts. It's highly unlikely that they are sabotaging you on purpose, they are just doing what feels right to them. It usually stems from years of cultural programming, an unconscious power struggle, or a tragic misunderstanding.

You have to let go of all of that. Release your expectations that they will understand and change and release the stress about the inevitable gifts. Besides, it would be unkind of you to take away the rush of pleasure that they get from gifting. Keep in mind that the delight that they are experiencing is a result of chemicals—dopamine + oxytocin—washing over their brain. So if that visual helps you, let them experience that hit of joy. Smile and let them have their moment.

Don't let the opening of gifts overwhelm you. Just because the gifts are being opened and the kids are saying "Wow!" and the Gift Giver is glowing as he or she receives hugs and "thank yous," it does not mean the gifts are now a permanent fixture in your strategically decluttered home.

If your children are very little, you can discreetly remove these toys from their room tomorrow, next week or next month (we'll discuss more on this in Chapter 9). If your children are older, you can discuss with them in advance of the holidays (probably while you are decluttering their room together, as mentioned in Chapter 3) the benefits of decluttering and minimalism. Discuss the fact that the Gift Giver will probably bring in more items than is necessary and that they will get to decide after Christmas which items they want to keep or donate. Perhaps they want to declutter more old belongings to make room for all of these new items. Or perhaps they can recognize that some of these new gifts would be better returned or donated. Use containers to set limits on the amount of belongings in their room (more on this in Chapter 3). Another option to consider is asking Gift Givers to keep any big or noisy toys at their own houses in a toy box for the children. They will love visiting and the Gift Giver will enjoy seeing their gift bring so much joy.

USE YOUR MANNERS

Remember that the goal of having a minimal, simple, intentional Christmas is to achieve peace in your home. Part of that is accepting that gifts and new items will enter your home, no matter how hard you try to stop it. So give yourself the gift of acceptance and give the Gift Giver your genuine gratitude.

Smile and say "thank you." Not only is this the classiest approach, but it will bring joy to both you and the Gift Giver. Let your own brain experience a rush of pleasure as you let yourself receive their message of love. That is all they are trying to do: Telling your family that they care for you. Accept that this is the way they know how to send that message and "hear" it. Give a hug, a kiss on the cheek, and a heartfelt "thank you." That is all that they really want, after all.

What you do with the items *after* Christmas is up to you. But for now, you are simply gracious.

Keep mentioning your decluttering purges throughout the year and spouting the benefits of having less. Perhaps you'll experience a Christmas where you see that they finally "get it."

9

SETTING UP YOUR
NEW NORMAL

It is my hope that you will see a drastic decrease in the influx of items entering your home this Christmas. The majority of this reduction will be due to your intentionality with preparation, budgeting, and setting limits (such as the 4-Gift Rule). If you opt-out of gift exchanges and decline invitations for social shopping, you will surely have less to sort through later. Hopefully, a portion of your friends and family understood your desire for less material items and you will be gifted less as well, despite a few avid gifters still showering you with their message of love.

You are the gatekeeper for what is allowed to enter your home, and you can decide where each new item must live once it has been granted permission to enter. After gifts have been unwrapped and the lovely fuss is made with paper and ribbons on the living room floor, there will be a natural time to begin cleaning up. Right away, you decide where items will make the most sense and declutter along the way.

As you put the newest teddy bear into the stuffed animal basket in your child's room, pluck one of the least-loved animals out of the basket. You decluttered this basket before Christmas, but you may realize that it is even easier to edit items out once you see the newer, shinier replacements. If you received a lovely new sweater for Christmas, then declutter the similar-looking, more worn sweater before you hang the new one up. That older sweater may have survived your earlier decluttering round before the holidays, but it has now been worn so much this season, that it is time to retire it. The newer, fluffier sweater will naturally be the top pick from now on. Procrastinating this step will lead to a huge decluttering project down the road, as items can very quickly build back up.

If this exercise—decluttering an older object before replacing it with the new item—seems too difficult, then perhaps the new object is not worthy of staying in your home. Just because the item was a thoughtful gift, does not mean that it has the right to drain your mental energy and physical space from now on. Be ruthless in this process. Question everything, as you are curating your house for a life of ease.

Determine why you think you should keep an item and question whether it is a valid enough reason for it to share space with you. Asking whether an item "sparks joy" is often not digging deep enough. People interpret "joy" in different ways, so try digging deeper. What is the source of the attachment?

Does it appear joyful because it was gifted to you by a loved one? Is it the thought of the loved one who gifted the item that actually kindles joy, or is it the item itself?

Or are you feeling beholden to a gift because of a feeling of guilt? It's a common emotion to feel guilty for getting rid of an object someone gave you, either because it cost them money, or their time, or even their thoughtful heart. Even still, it's not a good enough reason to hold on to a gift.

Another confusion of either joy or guilt is because of perceived value or sunk-cost bias. It can be terribly difficult to get rid of something that was once expensive. We either confuse the cost of the item with joy, or we remember how joyful we were at the moment we purchased it. On the flip side, we might simply feel too guilty to acknowledge the wastefulness of that purchase, so we hold on to an object to continue to "validate" its existence in our life.

There were many things that I decided "sparked joy" for me when I did my initial decluttering rounds. It was not until examining them further at later dates that I realized I was confusing joy with other emotions and psychological reasons for holding on.

There are two main questions I use now to test whether an item should remain. The first is: "Will I use this on a frequent basis?" Items that are actually used are an obvious keeper. These are the utilitarian necessary items to run a functional household. The next question addresses the problem with accumulating multiples of the same type of object: "Which one is the one I would grab first?"

To give an example, if someone gifted me a wine opener, I would determine that, yes, I would use this. Then I would examine all eight wine openers cluttering my kitchen drawer and think, if I had a guest bring a bottle of wine to my house, which one would I grab from this drawer to offer her? Would it be the silly wine opener I was just gifted that had a cutesy animal perched on top with "Bottoms Up!" engraved on it? Would it be the cheap hotel one that was given away as swag? Or would it be the classic, sturdy stainless steel one with the grips on the sides that allows you to effortlessly pull the cork up? The stainless steel one will always remain my favorite and the go-to that I naturally pick up first. Just because Aunt Sarah gifted me the silly animal wine opener which elicited a chuckle from everyone in the room on Christmas Day, and just because I love my Aunt Sarah so much, does not mean I'm beholden to this gift. Just because the cheap hotel one reminds me of a vacation we took five years ago, does not mean the memories of that vacation will be erased if I no longer own the hotel's free swag. The moment I realize this, I declutter seven of the eight wine openers, and feel relief at the sight of all that precious space my drawer has gained.

Clothing is particularly difficult to declutter for many of us. An example that has helped me is when I applied this same exercise to the large amount of "little black dresses" I once had accumulated. Since they are classics they can be dressed up or down and, unless there's a particularly trendy cut, they never really go out of style. I've purchased, been gifted, and inherited lovely second-hand versions of this classic dress.

Before long, I had probably 20 of these dresses—and they all still fit me, were in great shape, and most of them came from great designers and reputable boutiques. The perceived value in them had me clutching to each one. Many of them had lovely memories attached to them, some were gifted or inherited from dear friends, and some I had spent a pretty penny on. I love black dresses, so when I asked "Does this spark joy?" each one was answered with a resounding "Yes!" But the question: "Which one would I grab *first*?" helped me distill which one sparked the *most* joy. Considering that I'm no longer in the workforce, rarely attend fancy events, and am lucky if I get three date nights a year with my husband, there was no need to fill my closet with twenty "fancy" dresses. When the rare date night next occurred, I knew exactly which one my hand would land on first. If I happened to be surprised with another date night the following month, I knew which one would be the clear winner for another nice night out. By searching for this order in priority, I was able to get rid of 17 fantastic black dresses. Now, when it's time to get dressed for a special event, I experience no "decision fatigue," as I know that my more limited options to pull from are all items I absolutely love.

While this advice can help you with decluttering efforts at any time during the year, I want you to keep this top-of-mind as you begin finding a place for each new gift. It's the perfect opportunity to edit and curate your home.

After you've done this small decluttering exercise, and as you find a place for each new Christmas item in your home, you'll have grown stronger "decluttering muscles" and be ready to tackle much larger projects later in the year. If you already practiced minimalism before reading this book, then you may have done a lot of work to edit your home down to the most loved essentials. Christmas does not have to wreck all of your hard work.

When all is said and done, I hope you enter the New Year feeling at peace in your home. I hope that taking down the Christmas decorations is a quick, painless chore, and that each item finds ample space in the few boxes that you pack away. I hope that you feel a sigh of relief as you drop off another box of donations for a charity shop, filled with gratitude for the abundance in your life. I hope that you feel at ease with your bank account. I hope that you feel satisfied with the way you spent your time with your family. I hope that you smile as you think of each simple tradition you experienced together. I hope that your Christmas Day with extended family was equally as cheerful. I hope that you felt truly present with them, and didn't waste any time stressed, hurried or distracted.

Most of all, I hope that the lessons learned in this book are things that you can apply to your life, every day of the year!

Happy Holidays and Merry Christmas!
I hope you have a happy New Year!

Looking for more?

Are you curious to learn more about popular design trends and the trending aesthetics of minimalism during the holidays? Are you looking for some simple recipes for family traditions?

You can access the free bonus chapter that accompanies this book to get a foundation on trending minimal decor and recipes. Having a true minimalist Christmas is not about design, but many of us are drawn to minimalism because of it. I hope you enjoy perusing the elements that many people find soothing and peaceful during the holidays.

Visit
**www.megnordmann.com/
minimalist-christmas-bonus-chapter**
for more.

Let's stay in touch!

Meg Nordmann blogs about minimalism
and financial independence at
www.megnordmann.com

You can follow her at
@megnordmann
on Instagram and Twitter or
"Like" Meg Nordmann's author page
on Facebook.
You can also follow this book at
@minimalist_christmas on Instagram
for weekly motivation and inspiration.

Where are you reading this?

Take a photo with this book or ebook
wherever you are and share it with me! Tag
the book and add **#MinimalistChristmas**
to your hashtags so I can see where
you are enjoying this book. I hope it has
inspired you!

NOTES

_____

_____

_____

_____

_____

_____

_____

_____

_____

_____

_____

_____

_____

_____

_____

_____

_____

_____

_____

_____

_____

_____

_____

_____

_____

Manufactured by Amazon.ca
Bolton, ON

15263290R00074